U : P : D : A : T : E

Apartheid in South Africa
1987 Edition

David M. Smith

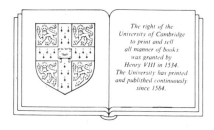

The right of the
University of Cambridge
to print and sell
all manner of books
was granted by
Henry VIII in 1534.
The University has printed
and published continuously
since 1584.

Cambridge

New York   New Rochelle   Melbourne   Sydney

Published by the Press Syndicate of the University of Cambridge

The Pitt Building, Trumpington Street, Cambridge CB2 1RP

32 East 57th Street, New York, NY10022, USA

10 Stamford Road, Oakleigh, Melbourne 3166, Australia

First published by Queen Mary College, University of London, in
December 1983.
First published by Cambridge University Press 1985.
Second edition 1987.

Printed in Great Britian by David Green Printers

British Library Cataloguing in Publication Data

Smith, David M. (David Marshall).
Apartheid in South Africa.   2nd ed   (Upadate).
1. Apartheid   South Africa   2. South Africa   Description
and travel   1966-
I. Title   II. Series
323.1'68   DT763

ISBN 0 521   33557 4 Second Edition
(ISBN   0   521   31586 7   First edition)

COVER

Part of Crossroads, the squatter settlement on the edge of Cape
Town.

U:P:D:A:T:E

The need to keep up to date with new trends and developments in geography or in aspects of geographical study is a constant problem for the teacher. This is particularly so where access to information on new techniques, ideas or sources of data is difficult and where contact with colleagues in higher education is limited. UpDate aims to improve this contact by providing brief, frequently revised booklets on topics directly linked to developments in the 'A' level syllabus and in college courses. They range from the compilation and interpretation of up-to-date statistical information of direct use in the classroom to the discussion of recent research work which may shed new light on the received ideas of the text-book. They are readable and cheap. Topics range over both physical and human geography, though coverage will reflect the specialisms of staff in the department of Geography and Earth Science at Queen Mary College where the series is produced.

John Eyles
Editor, UpDate

U:P:D:A:T:E updated

Apartheid in South Africa is the first in the UpDate series to be revised. The original edition was published in 1983 and much has happened in South Africa since then. The basic structure of the volume has been preserved, with the factual material updated from the latest available sources. The main features of this new edition are two new sections, on unrest and on the 'reform' of apartheid, which extend the scope of the work for educational use and should also be of interest to the general reader seeking up-to-date information on South Africa. The sections on the economy and urbanisation have also been extended. While every effort has been made to ensure the topicality and reliability of the material presented, it should be recognised that the censorship prevailing in South Africa at the time of writing (the beginning of 1987) has limited access to information on some subjects. There may also have been significant new developments since going to press.

David M. Smith

THE AUTHOR

David Smith is Professor of Geography at Queen Mary Colleg
University of London. He lived in South Africa for a ye
(1972-73) and held lecturing appointments at the University
Natal and the University of the Witwatersrand. He returned
South Africa in the summer of 1979, on a visit sponsored by t
Students' Union of the University of Cape Town.

Professor Smith's other academic appointments have been
the University of Manchester, Southern Illinois University, t
University of Florida, the University of New England (New Sou
Wales) and the Australian National University. He has also ma
a number of study visits to Eastern Europe.

Professor Smith has written or edited twelve books, in t
fields of economic and social geography. These inclu
Industrial Location: An Economic Geographical Analysis (197
Wiley, 2nd edition 1981), **Human Geography: A Welfare Approa**
(1977, Arnold), **Where the Grass is Greener: Living in an Unequ
World** (1979, Penguin), and **Living under Apartheid: Aspects**
Urbanization and Social Change in South Africa (1982, Allen a
Unwin). His latest book is **Geography, Inequality and Socie**
(1987, Cambridge University Press) which includes a case study
South Africa.

ACKNOWLEDGEMENTS

The author is grateful to Messrs. Allen and Unwin for permissi
to reproduce maps from his book **Living Under Apartheid** and to
number of the contributors to that volume for providing inform
tion which has been incorporated into the present publicatio
Dr A. Lemon provided a review of the manuscript of the fir
edition in draft and made some helpful suggestions. Denis Fai
Beverley Naidoo and others made helpful suggestions which ha
been incorporated into the revised edition. The South Afric
Institute of Race Relations kindly provided an advance copy
their latest **Survey of Race Relations in South Africa**. Car
Gray word-processed the revision and Leslie Milne was responsib
for new artwork and make-up of the manuscript.

CONTENTS

6

Plate 1   'Petty apartheid': seats marked for Whites only on the
Durban sea front in the early 197Cs. Most such signs
have now been removed.

Plate 2   Most beaches in South Africa are now integrated, but
racial segregation persists in Durban. The facilities
shown above (photographed in 1979) are for the
'Coloured Community', who could still not use 'White'
beaches in January 1987 when a Coloured member of
parliament broke the law in this respect in a public
demonstration (later apologising to the State
President).

1 The nature of apartheid

'If I were to wake up one morning and find myself a Black man, the only major difference would be geographical'.

B. J. Vorster, former Prime Minister of South Africa (quoted in the **Johannesburg Star**, 3 April 1973).

Township parents and pupils tackle a political dilemma

George Brock, Johannesburg

1987

bined to form a forcing house for new ideas. And so emerged "people's education".

Durban

Beach apartheid in slow retreat

When President Botha talks about the "total

change in use of public libraries: she received letters warning her that there would

PRISONERS OF CONSCIENCE

South Africa

Pretoria prohibits reports on ANC

From George Brock Port Elizabeth

Court test for Botha press laws

From George Brock Johannesburg

South Africa's two main English-language newspaper

Samuel Fezile

By Caroline Moorehead

Botha's white elections

Afrikaner right in trial of strength

Johannesburg — The key issue in the forthcoming South African

test of

ANC men out

Maputo (Reuter) — The representative of the African

South Africa's four million white voters only, who form about 18 per cent of the tion. Mr Botha has said ere would be no elec- o the Indian and Col- parliaments because

Coloured leader in clash with Botha over segregation

From Ray Kennedy, Johannesburg

ANC appeals to white South Africans to help it build a new nation

From George Brock, Lusaka

The African National Con-

Sanctions pressure fails to change Pretoria thinking

From Michael Hornsby, Johannesburg

Economic sanctions against South Africa have failed to

Most whites, it says, are sympathetic to the efforts being made by Pretoria to

Mrs Mandela detained in raid on home

Johannesburg — Mrs Win-

Fund will help frontline states apply sanctions

From Michael Hamlyn, Delhi

The Non-Aligned Movement yesterday gave a formal shape to the Africa Fund, which is aimed at helping the frontline African states to

Israelis

Political tensions in South Africa

Right wing taps white fears in bid to become Opposition

From George Brock, Randfontein

South African Indians tell Attenborough to stay away

leaders of the South Indian community

for Sir Richard Attenborough should not come week to attend the opening award-winning film which will be shown racially segregated

Ban on mixed marriages in South Africa to stay

Mr Louis South Africa and Order, Government that both being fully a

Only a few Botha, The Prime Minister,

1983

In the case of ch it is possible apply to the Government for collecting and to be shown to a mixture audience. This was not the however, in the case of Johannesburg premiere

S Africa rugby tour cancelled

The French rugby planned tour of South Africa was finally cancelled Y after President Mit- refused to reconsider to r of Diana Ogilvie at sporting contacts to be t of Albert Ferrasse, rugby on president said not did not win."

Staying away from S Africa

by two S Africa If there is one thi tain's pension fu nagers are not int ted in at the moment silling money into Sou rican investment art with, British inv traditionally ha proportionate holdin

Black journalist sent to jail

Johannesburg — A black journalist on the Government newspaper has been sentenced to two and a half years in prison for violating laws of the Afrikaans published by the Pan Y African Congress, Michael Molose. This journal

Pretoria to close city parks to blacks

From Michael Hornsby Johannesburg

Cape Town (Reuter) — Black squatters defied South Africa's influx control laws and camp outside their shacks at a camp that had been

MCC tour of S Africa would threaten game

CRICKET

body should be in any doubt the serious threat to organised s of rthat were so be a issue of

the reserves of British sportsmen, will be on the South Africa to see for man or either origin? by seeing that for himself he will not have to

Pretoria unveils long-awaited reforms

From Michael Hornsby, Johannesburg

The South African Government yesterday unveiled its long-awaited constitutional reforms, which if put into effect would give the country its first multiracial parliament, but keep ultimate control in white hands through the office of a new and powerful executive presidency reforms entitled the

parliament divided into three houses, one each for the country's 4.6 million whites, 2.7 million mixed-blood Coloured and 850,000 Asians (almost all Indian). Each house would be

would legislate separately for its own race group.

All other matters are considered to be "general affairs" and would have to be by a majority in eac The parliament won not be possi ance to be formed four lines to ou yority group in

Blacks at gold mine quit after violence

Cinemas hurt by Puttnam's apartheid lead

South Africa's unrest

Chanting black youths spark riots in Natal beach resorts

From Ray Kennedy, Johannesburg

Young blacks yelling African National Congress slogans set off what police last night described as scenes of "unprecedented violence" on a newly racially-integrated beach on South Africa's Natal coast south of Durban.

The sun-drenched Natal coastline is packed with scores

Umgababa beach, 20 miles south of Durban.

They said that about 8,000 people were on the beach when about 60 young blacks singing ANC anthems created "a hostile atmosphere".

By the time police arrived on the scene, a tearoom had been wrecked, four parked

said that a black man and woman were set on fire by about 20 people it described as "black radicals" in the Emdeni district of Soweto.

Another woman was burnt to death by about 90 blacks in the White City area of Soweto, the bureau said. Police found

Railway apartheid stays

From Michael Hornsby, Johannesburg

Strict apartheid will continue to be enforced on trains and in railway stations in South Africa, Mr Hendrik Schoeman, the Transport Minister, has told Parliament.

His statement conflicts with stated government policy to scrap what it terms "harmful" discriminatory measures.

Blacks in terrorism trial are acquitted

From Michael Hornsby Johannesburg

Four young black people, on trial for nine months on charges under the Terrorism Act, have been acquitted because the magistrate found that witnesses called by the state had given unreliable and contradictory evidence.

In the case of three witnesses the magistrate, Mr I. J. Luther, was satisfied that had been driven to statements they did not me give by the threats and of police under sharp actio

Mr Schoeman is consid- to be one of the most s ritof Botha.

Shift to right in Transvaal

Botha gets a racial thumbs down

From Michael Hornsby

South Africa's constitutional proposals for the first time give some political power and share rights with the coloured

Universities protest at race quotas

From Michael Hornsby, Johannesburg

The vice-chancellors of Sou Africa's four main Englis speaking universities ha and a strong joint protes tion legislation going throu liament which would for em to observe racially base zotas for the admissio lack students.

The protest was neve meeting aga after

Black power salutes at Transvaal funeral

From Michael Hornsby, Johannesburg

Mr Louis, th The black commun eader after the coloured with the results of a police Saturday, rest of the week

Coloureds quit

Johannesburg — The (APP) The South African Labour Party, comprising coloured people, decided to leave the white coloured Assembly and Blacks representative after

Black dies in police cell but his father survives electric torture

From Michael Hornsby, Johannesburg

P. W. Botha, the South as Prime Minister, prom- today and for a pr would press ahead

dead last week they were both taken to the duskardorp police station and the body of his son

his son was dead. He was also floor of his cell beside the

Botha presses on regardless

From Michael Hornsby, Johannesburg

1 THE NATURE OF APARTHEID

A black man shot dead; constitutional reforms proposed; a rugby tour cancelled, a cricket tour planned; a journalist jailed, 'terrorists' acquitted; mixed marriages remain banned, railway stations segregated and Pretoria reverts to the exclusion of blacks from city parks; Richard Attenborough stays away after the fuss over segregated audiences for the film Gandhi; constitutional reforms criticised; another black man dead. These were just a few of the stories about South Africa to appear in one British newspaper - The Times - during a month in 1983 when the first edition of this work was being prepared (see inset on opposite page). Four years on there are new stories, with South Africa even more in the news as growing internal unrest and external opposition to apartheid increases the pressure for change.

To many people the word apartheid evokes racial discrimination, backed up by a repressive police state. While there is some truth in this view it is simplistic, and fails to convey the full significance of apartheid. The interpretation of apartheid adopted here embraces a broad range of state policies and practices which pervade many aspects of South Africa's economy, society and polity. Apartheid also has a strong spatial element, appreciation of which is crucial to the comprehension of the geography of South Africa which is in important respects being recreated by government policy. The objective of this publication is to update understanding of apartheid as well as to present the latest available factual information.

/Apartheid is a unique feature of a distinctive history, which has left South Africa with a high degree of racial, ethnic and cultural diversity./ White settlement began with the arrival of Jan van Riebeeck in 1652 to set up a base for the Dutch East India Company at Cape Town, but it was the British occupation of the Cape at the beginning of the nineteenth century and their immigration into Natal which really consolidated white control. While the indigenous black population of the Cape was small, much larger numbers were encountered in the interior, especially when the Great Trek took Boer descendants of the early Dutch settlers eastwards and northwards into what is now the Orange Free State, the Transvaal and northern Natal. /A growing so-called 'coloured' population was generated by miscegenation between colonisers, the indigenous people, and Malays brought in as slaves./ Further variety was introduced into South Africa's population in the latter part of the nineteenth century, with the Indians imported to work the Natal sugar fields.

There are four race groups officially recognised in South Africa. These are Blacks, Whites, Coloureds and Asians./ The Blacks comprise the indigenous African negro population, known officially as the 'Bantu' until this pejorative term was abandoned in the 1970s. In liberal circles, Africans is usually preferred to the official description Blacks. The situation is further complicated by the fact that members of all 'non-white' groups are increasingly referring to themselves collectively as blacks. The term Blacks with an initial capital letter is used

in this publication to denote the more restricted official usag
The Whites are made up mostly of people of British or Dut
descent; the latter, the Afrikaners, comprise almost 60 per ce
of the total White population. Most of the Coloureds share wi
the Afrikaners their native language of Afrikaans. The Asian
usually referred to as Indians, are descended almost entire
from people from the Indian sub-continent.

Racial nomenclature poses difficult and controversial que
tions in South Africa, for it can be argued that to accept t
offical terms is to assist in giving legitimacy to the aparthe
system. In this publication the four official terms are adopt
simply because most of the data presented come from offici
sources, though the terms Africans and Indians are used in so
places as synonymous with Blacks and Asians respectively. Refe
ences to parts of South Africa as 'White' denote an offici
connotation, without implying that such a description is eith
legitimate or accurate in a factual sense. The use of quotati
marks in connection with certain other terms, such as 'hom
lands', indicates an official term which derives its meaning fr
the apartheid system itself - as will be explained in subseque
discussions.

The distribution of population by race group is shown
Table 1.1. The Blacks are in a large majority; the Whit
comprise the second largest group, exceeding the Coloureds a
Asians taken together by about one million. The two sets
figures for 1985 are explained by the fact that the offici
definition of the Republic of South Africa (RSA) excludes t
'TBVC' areas - the Transkei, Bophuthatswana, Venda and Ciskei
to which the South African government has granted a form
independence (see below, page 11). The result is a reduction
the Black share of the population and a comparable increase
the Whites' share, when compared with the original definition
the national territory (referred to as South Africa in th
publication to distinguish it from the official Republic of Sou
Africa).

Apartheid is a response to the population distribution sho
in Table 1.1 - to the numerical supremacy of Blacks (and others
in a land controlled by the Whites. Apartheid means apartness
separation in Afrikaans, and the essence of the policy of apa
theid is the social and spatial separation of the major rac
groups. This policy operates at three geographical scales
nationally, within the cities or towns, and with respect to t
use of particular facilities. The basic principle is that rac
groups are assigned particular territory for what is suppose
ultimately to be their exclusive occupance. However, the imple
mentation of this principle differs significantly at the nationa
and local (city) levels. What follows refers to the grand desig
attributed largely to former Primary Minister Dr H. F. Verwoerd
elaboration of apartheid in the 1950s and early 1960s, much
which remains in place today despite some 'reforms' (see Chapte
10).

e 1.1 Population by race group 1960-1985

| | South Africa | | | | | | | | RSA | |
| | 1960 | | 1970 | | 1980 | | 1985 | | 1985 | |
p	No 1000s	% of total	No 1000s	% of total	No 1000s	% of total	No 1000s	% of total	No 1000s	% of total
ks	10,928	68.3	15,340	70.4	20,886	72.5	21,197	72.0	15,243	65.0
es	3,080	19.3	3,773	17.3	4,528	15.6	4,591	15.6	4,577	19.5
ureds	1,509	9.4	2,051	9.4	2,613	9.0	2,854	9.7	2,825	12.1
ns	477	3.0	630	2.9	821	2.9	802	2.7	794	3.4
l	15,994	100.0	21,794	100.0	28,848	100.0	29,444	100.0	23,439	100.0

ce: Census of Population 1960, 1970, 1980 and 1985 (preliminary figures). The 1980 figures for South Africa
include an estimate from the Bureau for Economic
Development, Cooperation and Research (BENSO) for the
population of the then 'independent republics' of
Transkei, Bophuthatswana and Venda. The 1985 figures
for South Africa include figures for the 'independent'
Transkei, Bophuthatswana, Venda and Ciskei from the
Development Bank of Southern Africa, reported in SAIRR
(1986, 1-2).

At the national level the territory of South Africa is divi-
simply between the Whites and the Blacks, such that the
es have almost 87 per cent of the total surface area (for
per cent of the population in 1985) and the Blacks a little
13 per cent (for 72.0 per cent of the population). The
k areas form a crescent around South Africa's major metro-
tan region of the Witwatersrand (Figure 1.1). When the South
can government introduced its policy of 'separate develop-
' in the 1950s, the areas allocated for the Blacks were
ed 'homelands', to denote the supposed association between
ers of the various African tribes and their traditional areas
rigin. The derogatory term 'Bantustan' was preferred in some
ters. The idea was that the 'homelands' set aside for each
he major tribal groups would eventually become independent in
rmal political sense, leaving the Whites in complete control
he rest of South Africa (i.e. the RSA).

The progress of this plan is indicated in Figure 1.1. Here a
inction is made between the four 'independent republics' as
South African government terms them, and the remaining six
k 'national states'. The Transkei was the first to be grant-
he status of 'sovereign independent state', in 1976, and this
followed by Bophuthatswana (1977), Venda (1979) and Ciskei
1). However, their independence has not been recognised by
United Nations, or indeed by any other country except the

12

Republic of South Africa. The remaining six 'homelands' have all
been granted 'full internal self-government' within the RSA. The
objective is eventually to turn them into independent republics,
though this move is not necessarily welcomed and in some cases is
being strongly resisted by the leaders of the 'states' themselves.

There are no 'homelands' or specific territorial allocations
for the Coloureds and Indians at the national level. They will
continue to reside in 'White' South Africa, i.e. the RSA.

The Coloureds and Indians do, however, have their allotted
space within the towns and cities of South Africa, along with the
Blacks and Whites. The Group Areas Act of 1950 gave legal status
to residential segregation and in 1950 a register was instituted
for the classification of the entire adult population according
to race or ethnic group. These two measures together provide for
the planned perpetuation and indeed strengthening of segregation
in urban areas. 'Group areas' are defined for the exclusive
occupation of specific races, and personal classification deter-
mines where any individual or family may and may not live.

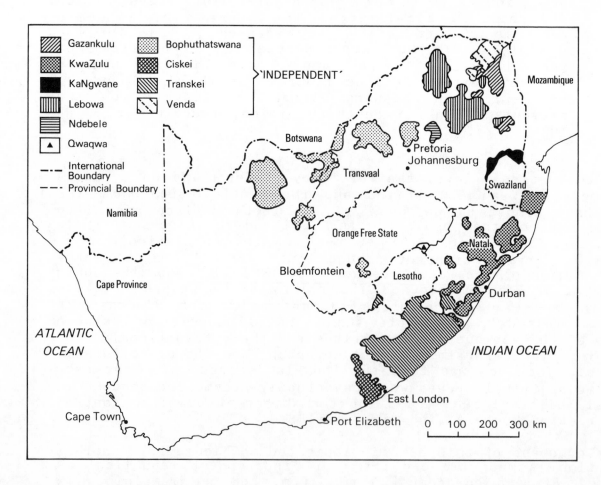

Figure 1.1   Apartheid at the national scale.   Black or African
'homelands' ('national states' and 'independent
republics') are shown according to the South African
government's 1975 consolidations proposals
Source: Smith (1982, p. 26)

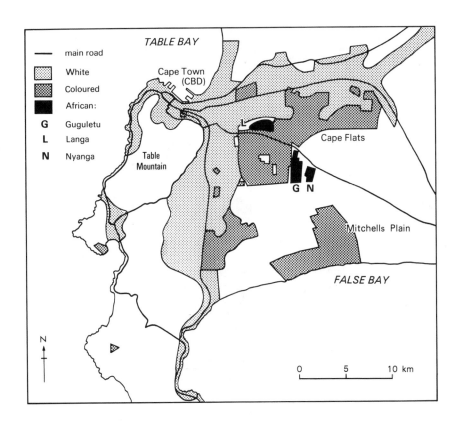

ure 1.2   Residential areas for different race groups in the
           Cape Town metropolitan area
           Source: based on Dewar and Ellis (1979, p. 59)

Figure 1.2 provides an example of the emerging pattern of
ial residential areas. Cape Town is the traditional home of a
ge proportion of South Africa's Coloureds (the term Cape
oureds is still sometimes used), and large areas are set aside
 them in the Cape Flats and a new town called Mitchells Plain
anned population about 0.25 million); a further new town of
antis (to house about 0.5 million Coloureds) is being con-
ucted 40 kms north of Cape Town.   The 'group areas' for Whites
lude the inner parts of the city and the attractive residen-
l districts along the eastern flank of Table Mountain.   There
 also three townships for Blacks.   The Coloureds outnumber
tes and Blacks together in the Cape Peninsula (Table 1.2).

A second example is shown in Figure 1.3.   Durban has the
gest Indian population of all South African cities; they
ily outnumber the Whites (Table 1.2).   As with the 'group
as' for Coloureds in Cape Town, those for Asians in Durban are
ipheral, while the areas for Whites include the central part
 the city and the axis out through Pinetown along the main
te inland.   Figure 1.3 shows two different kinds of areas for
cks - townships in the city itself or part of Natal, and much
ger townships in the 'homeland' of KwaZulu (i.e. Umlazi and
Mashu).   The KwaZulu townships are effectively part of metro-
itan Durban and many of their residents commute into the city
ly (see Chapter 6), yet officially they belong to another
te which it is intended will ultimately be made independent of
 RSA.   A radical proposal to merge Natal (including Durban)
KwaZulu was rejected by the government in 1986.

14

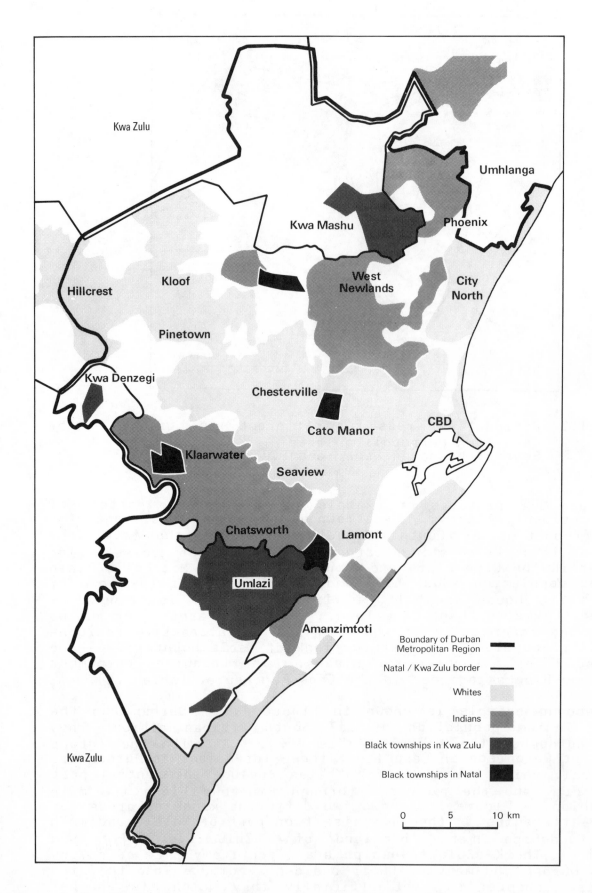

Kwa Zulu

Umhlanga

Kwa Mashu

Phoenix

West
Newlands

City
North

Kloof

Hillcrest

Pinetown

Kwa Denzegi

Chesterville

CBD

Cato Manor

Klaarwater

Seaview

Chatsworth

Lamont

Umlazi

Amanzimtoti

Boundary of Durban
Metropolitan Region

Natal / Kwa Zulu border

Whites

Indians

Black townships in Kwa Zulu

Black townships in Natal

Kwa Zulu

0   5   10 km

Figure 1.3   Residential areas for different race groups in the
             Durban metropolitan region
             Source: Based in part on map prepared by E. Harrhoff,
             courtesy G. Maasdorp

Table 1.2   Population of major urban areas 1980 by race group
           (1000s)

Urban Area	Blacks	Whites	Coloureds	Asians	Total
Johannesburg	1026	541	106	53	1726
Cape Peninsula	172	484	820	15	1491
Durban/Pinetown	117	320	56	468	961
East Rand	550	264	19	15	848
Pretoria	322	386	14	14	736
Port Elizabeth/ Uitenhage	279	159	140	7	585
West Rand	309	187	12	4	512

Source: 1980 Census (provisional figures). The Black population
          is probably a substantial underestimate of the true
          figure, including illegal residents, in most cities.

     The situation of the Blacks in South African cities requires
further clarification.   Officially the entire Black population
belongs to one or other of the 'homelands' (Black 'states' or
'republics'), in the sense that it is here that they are supposed
to exercise their political rights and take their citizenship.
However, half the Black population of South Africa actually lives
in the 'White' areas (see below, Chapter 4), most of them in the
cities.   Rights to reside in an urban area were until recently
governed primarily by Section 10 of the Black (Urban Areas)
Consolidation Act, which stated that an African may claim permanent residence in an urban area only if he had lived there
continously since birth, had been lawfully there continuously for
15 years, or had worked there for the same employer for 10 years.
A policy of 'orderly urbanisation' has now been introduced for
the settlement of Africans, previously controlled by the so-
called Pass Laws, which required documentary evidence of their
'Section 10' rights to be in the 'White' city (see Chapter 7).

     In addition to spatial separation, apartheid enshrines in law
the traditional practices of strict racial segregation of a wide
range of public and private facilities.   Although this 'petty
apartheid' has been reduced in recent years it still applies, in
early 1987, to some beaches, buses, cinemas, hotels and restaurants.   The first relaxations came in the 1970s, when 'White'
facilities could admit Blacks, Indians and Coloureds by acquiring
'international' status from the government.   However, racial
mixing in 'international' hotels, for example, was greatly
limited by the fact that there is very little basis for inter-
racial social contact in everyday life.   While some integration
has been achieved in sport, this again is greatly restricted by

16

residential segregation and the traditional social distan
between the races. Petty apartheid is proving to be the easie
field for reform, although there is also some assault on t
concept of 'group areas' (Chapter 1C).

Although informal and to some extent formal segregation has
long tradition in South Africa, it is one political party - t
Nationalists - who have been responsible for the legal structu
on which racial separation now rests. Since assuming power
194E, the Nationalists have increased their share of seats
parliament - from 70 out of 150 to 133 out of 178 in 1987. T
main opposition, the United Party, was dissolved in 1977 a
replaced by the Progressive Federal Party which is similar in i
'verligte' (enlightened) orientation to the old Progressi
Party. In 1982 a group of MPs left the Nationalists to form
new Conservative Party, which has replaced the Herstig
Nationale as the main opposition on the 'verkrampte' or hard-li
racist end of the political spectrum. The number of votes ca
and seats won in the 1987 election compared with 1981 are sho
in Table 1.3. The voting strength of the Conservative Par
should be noted, as they pose a major challenge to t
Nationalists from the right. The much publicised defection
three liberal Nationalists who stood as Independent candidat
yielded one seat. The shift to the right in 1987 made t
Conservatives the official opposition, replacing the PFP.

In 1983 Prime Minister P. W. Botha unveiled constitution
'reforms' which provided for a new parliament with three houses
one each for the Coloureds and Asians as well as the White
There was to be no representation for Blacks, and power was
remain firmly in White hands. Opposition to the new proposa
came from both ends of the political spectrum, but in Novemb
1983 the constitution was approved by 66 per cent of Whit
voting in a referendum, and in 1984 the first elections to t
Coloured and Asian houses were held. The new constitution
considered further in Chapter 1C.

Table 1.3   General election results and White parliamentary
            seats, 1981 and 1987

Party	Votes		Seats	
	1981	1987	1981	1
National	778,371	1,075,508	131	1
Conservative	-	547,559	-	
Progressive Federal	265,297	288,574	26	
New Republic	93,603	40,494	8	
Herstigte Nasionale	191,294	61,456	0	
Others	21,413	27,149	0	

Source: RSA (1983, pp. 160-1); The Times, 9 May 1987

2 Racial inequality

18

Plate 3   How the other one-seventh lives: a White suburb of
           Johannesburg.   Note the servants' huts adjoining the
           houses or in the gardens.

Plate 4   House in an upper income suburb of Cape Town, complete
           with tennis court, swimming pool and beautiful garden,
           and well protected from the other six-sevenths.

2 RACIAL INEQUALITY

Inequality among the races is an inevitable feature of apartheid. This applies not only to the freedom to live where one chooses, to vote where one lives, to use 'public' facilities and so on, but also to a wide variety of economic and social conditions.

The most obvious manifestation of inequality is the distribution of income by race group, when compared with population. The latest available figures (for 1977) show 26 per cent of national income going to the Blacks who comprise 72 per cent of the population, 64 per cent going to the Whites (16 per cent of the population), and the Coloureds and Asians receiving 7 and 3 per cent of income respectively. A comparison with earlier figures shows only a very small reduction in inequality of income distribution in recent years.

Table 2.1 lists figures for the four race groups on a range of economic and social indicators along with ratios for Whites to Blacks (W : B). The advantage of the Whites varies from just over 2:1 for pupils per teacher to almost 60:1 for the tuberculosis rate. The infant mortality rate among Blacks outside 'White' areas is unknown as many births and deaths are not registered, but a figure well in excess of 100 per 1000 live births is likely. The Coloureds and Asians occupy positions between the Whites and Blacks, with Asians generally having a marked advantage.

Table 2.1 Selected economic and social indicators by race

Indicator	Blacks	Whites	Coloureds	Asians	W : B
Average monthly household income (R) 1985	352	1958	680	1109	5.59
Maximum monthly social pensions (R) 1984[+]	65	166	103	103	2.55
Infant deaths/1000 births 1985 ('White' areas)	80	13	60	24	16.15
Tuberculosis cases / 100,000 popn 1979*	779.9	13.5	185.0	15.0	57.77
Non-capital expenditure on school pupils/capita (R) 1984–85	227	1702	693	1112	7.50
Pupils per teacher 1985 ('White' areas)	41.2	18.7	25.4	22.5	2.20

Source: SAIRR (1986) except* from SAIRR (1981) and[+] from SAIRR (1985)

Note: The South African Rand (R) exchanges at R3.00 = £1.00 (1987)

   Table 2.2 provides details of racial differences in earnin
in various sectors of the economy. Again, the Whites are mark
edly better off than the others, especially the Blacks, while th
Asians do somewhat better than the Coloureds in every sector
Only in electricity do earnings of Blacks come anywhere nea
those of the Coloureds.

   An important question is how far the gap between the races i
narrowing. Some evidence with respect to earnings in differen
sectors of the economy is provided by Table 2.2. A comparison o
the increases over the decade 1973-1983 shows greater improve
ments for the Coloureds, Asians and Blacks than for the Whites
This is most marked with respect to the Blacks, whose improve
position reflects both internal agitation for higher wages on th
part of Black workers and external (overseas) pressure on employ
ers. The ratios of White to Black earnings have been reduced i
every sector, the more so in services and, quite dramatically, i
mining. However, the gaps remain substantial and in most sector
it would take some decades to eliminate them altogether even i
the unlikely event of the pace of relative improvement in Blac
earnings during the 1970s continuing to be maintained.

Table 2.2 Average monthly earnings by race in various sectors o
the economy 1973 and 1983

Sector	Earnings (R) 1983				1983 : 1973				W
	B	W	C	A	B	W	C	A	1973
Mining	277	1491	484	732	9.6	3.1	4.7	5.5	16.4
Manufacturing	346	1402	393	483	4.7	3.6	3.8	4.4	5.5
Electricity	384	1318	415	543	4.8	3.1	3.6	-	5.3
Construction	280	1428	454	763	3.9	3.5	3.2	4.1	7.2
Trade and accommodation	231	931	329	493	3.9	3.6	3.7	4.1	4.4
Transport and communications	354	1283	391	1066	5.2	3.6	3.9	7.7	5.3
Finance and insurance	451	1096	562	764	4.8	3.2	4.4	4.0	3.6
Government and services	295	1107	437	780	4.8	3.2	3.3	4.6	5.7

Source: RSA (1985, p. 485); - = no data for 1973

Of course income and other conditions vary within the race groups
as well as between them. The Asians and (to a lesser extent)
Coloureds have emerging middle-classes supplementing the small
business elite which has always existed in the Indian community,
and their level of living is sharply differentiated from that of
the rest of these race groups. Even among the Blacks there is a
small group of rich business and professional people in the townships. There are some poor Whites, though protected employment
(e.g. in public utilities) and 'job reservation', which until
recently preserved certain occupations for Whites, ensure them a
living standard superior to that of most people in the other race
groups.

The results of a survey of 8CC African families and the same
number of Whites permits a comparison of the proportion of households in different income brackets (Figure 2.1). For both the
national sample and the (generally richer) Johannesburg residents
there is little overlap between the two distributions (ie very
few Black households earn more than the poorest Whites), though
they both cover a wide range of incomes.

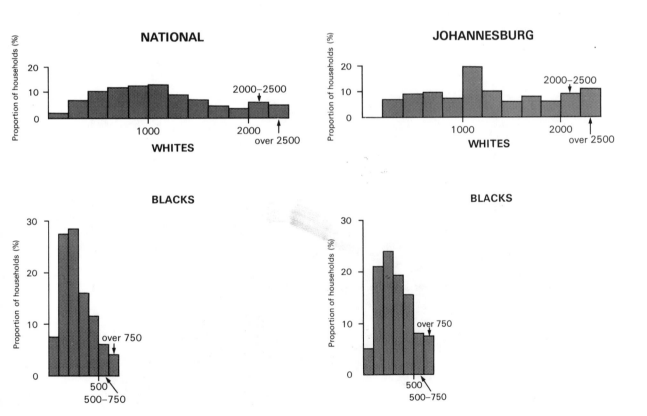

Figure 2.1   Income distribution among samples of Black and White
             families in 1981
             Source: SAIRR (1982, p. 114)

Plate 5   House of a well-to-do Indian family in Lenesia, the Indian township on the southern edge of greater Johannesburg.

Plate 6   Evidence of a small property-owning bourgeoisie in Bophuthatswana - a fine home built by the proprietor of the adjoining shop and bar.

3   Creating apartheid

Plate 7   Part of District Six near the centre of Cape Town.
District Six has a long association with the Coloured
community but has been largely cleared under the Group
Areas Act.

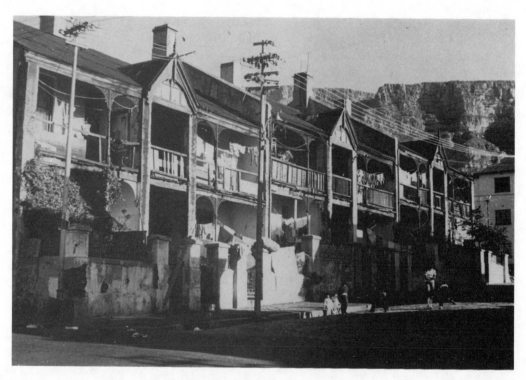

Plate 8   Old cottage property in District Six, with Table
Mountain in the background. Such property is often
'Chelseafied' when reoccupied by Whites after the
Coloureds have been moved out.

3 CREATING APARTHEID

The creation of racial residential segregation at the national
and city scales has required the relocation of large numbers of
people.   Accurate figures are difficult to obtain, but a recent
estimate cited by the Black Sash Organisation puts it at approximately 3 million people from 1960 to 1980, while a study by the
Surplus People Project arrives at a figure of 3.5 million for the
past 20 years.   Table 3.1 shows the number of people (mostly
Blacks) involved in various types of removals or relocations
according to this last study.   The first category refers to
changes in the way in which Africans could work on the land in
'White' South Africa.   Under the Natives' Land Act of 1913,
Africans hiring, leasing or owning land outside their scheduled
'reserves' (which later became the 'homelands') were said to be
squatting illegally in 'White' areas.   Subsequently large numbers
of squatters and labour tenants (working part of the year for
white farmers in return for land and grazing rights) have been
resettled in the reserves or 'homelands' - a process accelerated
by agricultural mechanisation in the 1950s and 1960s.

The term 'black spots' describes parcels of land bought
freehold by Africans before the 1913 Act.   The elimination of
'black spots' is an important feature of the consolidation of the
'homelands'.   As the land involved has often been owned and
farmed by the same Black families for generations, the forced
resettlement of the inhabitants of 'black spots' in what can be a
far distant 'homeland' is a source of great hardship.   The number
affected approaches 0.7 million.   Almost 1 million Africans are
subject to removal from the remaining 'black spots' and other
areas, under the 1975 proposals to reduce the number of separate
'homeland' territorial units from over 100 to less than 30.

Figure 3.1 illustrates the process of Black resettlement, in
connection with the territorial consolidation of the Tswana
people into the 'homeland' of Bophuthatswana - now officially an
'independent republic'.   Some of the distances moved are well
over 100 miles.   Population relocation can also involve the
transfer of people living in the 'homelands' but of the "wrong"
tribe.   Examples on the map are the removal of non-Tswanas from
the section of Bophuthatswana north of Pretoria to the Ndebele
'homeland' and from Thaba Nchu to the Qwaqwa 'homeland'.

In the urban areas the demolition of old townships and informal (squatter) settlements has resulted in the relocation of
large numbers of Blacks (see Table 3.1).   Some have been rehoused
in new townships, others relocated in the 'homelands'.   Blacks
may also be removed from 'White' cities if they become 'unpro-
ductive' (e.g. too old or ill to work) or otherwise lose their
residence rights, and in cases where they become officially
'undesirable', e.g. political activists.

During the 1980s Black removals have continued at a level of
20-30,000 per year.   In mid-1986 the government announced that it
would not proceed with hundreds of thousands of outstanding
removals, but there is evidence that resettlement is continuing.

26

Table 3.1   Population affected by removal or relocation c.
            1960-1980

Type of removal	Numbers
Eviction of Black tenants, squatters and surplus labour from 'white' farmland	1,129,000
Clearance of 'black spots', and 'homeland' consolidation	674,000
Urban relocation and removal from 'White' areas to 'homeland' townships	670,000
Removal from unauthorised (spontaneous) urban settlements	112,000
'Group area' removals arising from racial re-zoning	834,400
Relocation due to development schemes and clearing sensitive areas	23,500
Political moves such as banishment and flight from oppression	50,000
Others	30,000
Total	3,522,900

Source: The Surplus People Project, as reported in Race Rela
         tions News (SAIRR), May/June 1983

Note: Some of these figures may be underestimates; for exampl
         other evidence suggests a larger number of peopl
         affected by removal from informal settlements.
         Stellenbosch University study in 1986 reported at leas
         4 million Blacks relocated into 'homelands' between 195
         and 1980.

     The creation of racially homogenous 'group areas' in th
cities has affected all race groups - the more so those who ar
not Whites. By 31 December 1984, 448 'group areas' had bee
proclaimed for the occupation of Whites, 313 for Coloureds an
116 for Indians (Black residential areas are 'townships', no
'group areas' in the strict sense). Table 3.2 shows something o
the impact, borne disproportionately by the Coloureds and Indian
with few Whites affected. The impact on Indian traders move
from areas proclaimed for Whites has been severe. People affect
ed by Group Area Act relocations include one-third of the entir
Indian population and one-sixth of the Coloureds; the total no
exceeds 800,000 (Table 3.1).

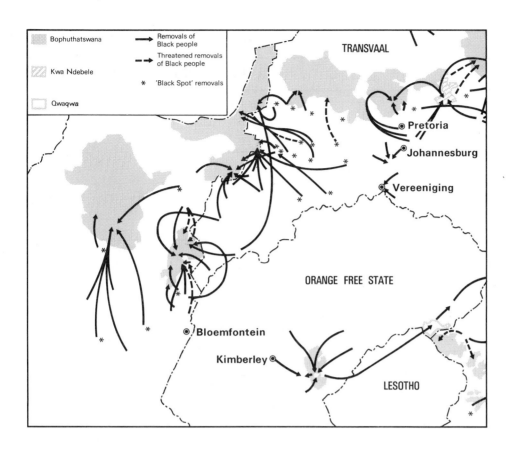

re 3.1   Relocation of Black/African population in the terri-
          torial consolidation of Bophuthatswana
          Source: section of map in Walt (1982)

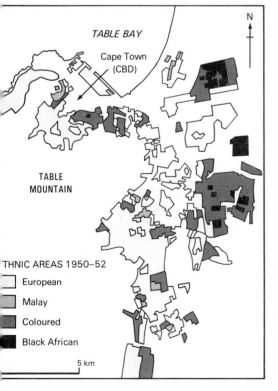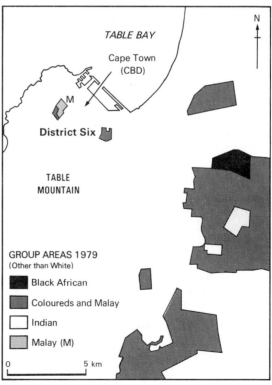

re 3.2   The distribution of ethnic groups in Cape Town 1950-
          52 and 'group areas' as defined in 1979
          Source: Western (1981, p. 51, p. 104)

Table 3.2 Families and traders affected by Group Area Act

Category	Whites	Coloureds	Indians
Families moved, up to 31 August 1984	2,418	83,691	40,067
Families remaining to be moved at 31 August 1984	258	3,790	2,366
Traders resettled up to 31 August 1984	54	187	2,530

Source: SAIRR (1986, pp. 348-49)

Two cases may be used to illustrate the impact of the creation of 'group areas'. The first concerns Cape Town, where the
broad pattern of racial residential space was illustrated in
Figure 1.2 above. Figure 3.2 shows the highly diverse ethnic
residential pattern in 1950-52, at the beginning of the apartheid
era, emphasising in particular the intermingling of small
Coloured and Malay enclaves within the predominantly White area
around the foot of Table Mountain. The 'group areas' for those
other than Whites show most of the old Coloured and Malay areas
eliminated and their population moved into the Cape Flats. All
that remains is the historic Malay Quarter to the south-west of
the CBD and Walmer Estate on the edge of District Six.

District Six (named after the old sixth district of Cape
Town) has become symbolic of the impact of the Group Areas Act.
It was closely associated with the history and culture of the
Coloured people and at one time had a population of about 60,000.
In 1966 District Six was proclaimed White under the Group Areas
Act, a move which was imposed by the National government in
Pretoria over the objection of the City of Cape Town. Most of
the area has subsequently been cleared, its houses demolished and
its population relocated. In 1979 District Six was officially
renamed Zonnebloem, as if to complete the elimination of its
former existence and identity.

The second case is from Durban, the 'group areas' of which
were shown in Figure 1.3 above. Before the era of apartheid the
Whites and Indians occupied their own highly segregated residential areas, with the Whites concentrated along the Berea ridge to
the west of the CBD and the Indians just beyond. Within the CBD
the Indians had their own mixed residential and commercial area
based on Grey Street (Figure 3.3). The designation of "group
areas" for the Indians has broken up their old communities and
forced them into more peripheral locations, leaving the central
parts of the city firmly in White control. Whereas most Indians
originally lived on freehold land, most now live in council
housing. There has also emerged a form of socio-economic segregation which hardly existed before; now the better-off Indians
have their own separate areas of fine homes, distinct from those
of the large majority.

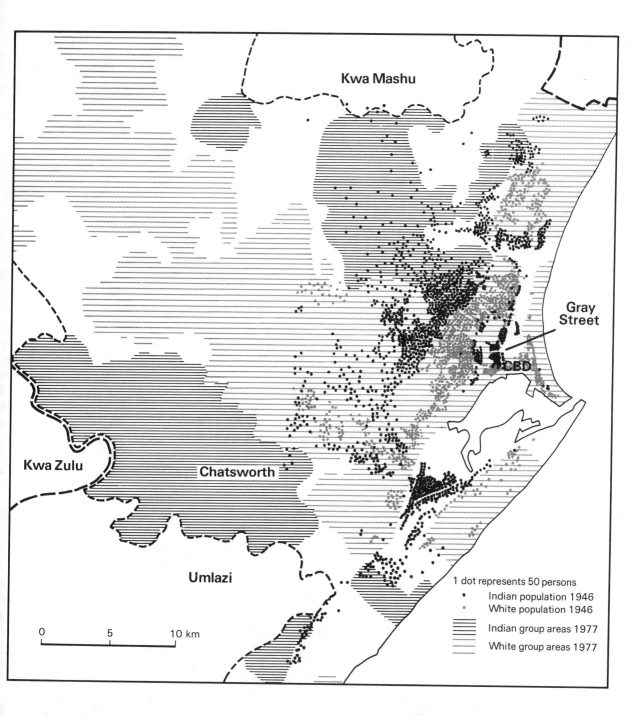

Figure 3.3 The distribution of the Indian population in Durban 1949 in relation to present 'group areas'
Source: Maasdorp and Pillay (1977, 24)

The fate of the Grey Street business district is similar in some respects to that of District Six. The Whites have always been concerned about competition from Indian traders and various formal and informal means were used to protect White businesses before the apartheid era. Grey Street represented Indian business success in a conspicuous inner-city location. In 1973 Grey

Street was proclaimed an area for Indian businesses but not f
residence. The significance of the distinction was that mar
businesses were family-run and residential accommodation wa
often integral (literally, over the shop); thus the viability c
Indian business was threatened indirectly. Between 1973 and 198
the resident population of the Grey Street area dropped fro
13,000 to 6,500, with implementation of the business-only pro
clamation, and the area's character has changed accordingly.

Population removals under the Group Areas Act are ofte
justified by the South African government as slum clearance. Th
quality of housing into which people are moved may be superior
some respects to the original, but there may be a loss of broade
community and environmental quality. For example, in the Cap
Flats human relationships are considered more impersonal, socia
deprivation more evident and personal safety less secure than
the traditional Coloured areas of Cape Town. In some of thes
areas housing was structurally sound if superficially delap.
dated, and the Group Areas Act has generated benefits for sor
Whites in a process referred to as 'Chelseafication', whereb
former Coloured homes are bought up cheaply and renovated t
create fashionable White residential areas.

There is increasing evidence of infringements of stric
residential segregation required by the 'group areas', with sor
cities turning a blind eye to the integration of certain neigh
bourhoods (Chapter 10). The Group Areas Act is a growing targe
for 'reform' but the government remains committed to separat
residential areas.

Plate 9   'Sub-economic' or subsidised rental property fc
            Coloureds in Cape Town. Such areas differ little frc
            the Black townships.

te 10   New accommodation for Coloureds in the Cape Flats.
         People relocated from District Six and other tradi-
         tional Coloured neighbourhoods now live in these con-
         ditions.

te 11   Mitchells Plain outside Cape Town, where a city of a
         quarter of a million is being built for Coloureds to
         encourage private home ownership.

Friends and neighbours

The kind of people who are buying houses at Mitchells Plain are the kind of people you would be glad to have as friends and neighbours. They are all people just like yourself who want to live a clean decent life – taking a pride in your home and garden; bringing up your children to appreciate the better things in life; helping each other in a spirit of fellowship; getting together for discussions, entertainment, Church and Club activities, etc.

A healthy new life for your children

Mitchells Plain is a place where your children will learn self-respect and self-confidence because they will be living away from crime and free from fear – mixing with clean-living children at School, Sports, Cubs, Scouts, Guides, Sunday School gatherings – the kind of life where they will feel encouraged to take part in activities which are for the good of the whole community.

THERE'S ROOM FOR YOU NOW!

There is no waiting li. You can move in witl one week.

Come and see Mitchells Plai Show Houses open all week

For further details PHONE 699550

Move to

Mitchel Plain

HEDLEY

Brochure advertising the new town for Coloureds at Mitchells Plain – there is room for them there, provided that they are Coloured.

4 Explaining apartheid

An analogy of apartheid, suggesting the white appropriation of the riches generated by black labour. The Whites enjoy a high standard of living returning little to the inhabitants of the 'homelands' across the fence. From a cartoon in the **Daily Mirror**, 6 March 1961, redrawn by Melanie Ward.

A harmonious relationship between South Africa and its landlocked neighbour Lesotho is portrayed here. The Highland Water Project due to be undertaken jointly promises thousands of jobs for Lesotho, but it is water for South Africa that is featured in this cartoon from the Afrikaans newspaper **Die Transvaler**, 1 October 1986. (The straw hat from Lesotho being handed to President Botha is labelled 'water project' in Afrikaans.)

4 EXPLAINING APARTHEID

As was indicated at the outset, an objective of this publication is to update understanding of apartheid as well as factual information. Media coverage of South Africa tends to focus on such features as petty apartheid, sports boycotts and police brutality, and this encourages a superficial and unduly narrow interpretation. Apartheid cannot be explained simply as race discrimination arising from antipathy between Blacks and Whites. South Africa itself cannot be dismissed simply as a repressive police state. The South African government operates with far more sophistication than is often supposed, and to a more complex purpose than simply keeping races apart or the Blacks in their place. Three different explanations for apartheid will be summarised briefly - the official government view, an interpretation which emphasises racial domination, and one which sees labour exploitation as the key. These explanations are not mutually exclusive nor do they cover all possible views, but they are broadly representative of the main alternative contemporary perspectives.

The official rationale sees territorial and social separation as the only way of preserving inter-racial harmony and the cultural integrity of each group. The term apartheid is now so pejorative as to be no longer part of the official lexicon. It was replaced some years ago by 'separate development' and more recently by 'multinational development'. Official terminology may change, but the basic principle of national-scale apartheid remains. South Africa's **Official Yearbook** (RSA, 1983, p. 195) says of the policy:

Today, it is a comprehensive programme designed to do justice to all the peoples of South Africa, providing as it does for economic cooperation and interdependence between Black and White, coupled with the highest possible degree of political freedom and self-determination for all in the peculiar circumstances of the country.

The 'homelands' policy is explained as follows in a book entitled **Homelands**, issued by the government-sponsored Bantu Investment Corporation (1979, p. 1):

Since it is the policy of the White government that the Black nations for which it still acts as guardian should eventually be able to exercise the right to full national independence, it is evident that the final geopolitical division of the Republic of South Africa lies at some point in the future. The progressive political development of the Republic's Black peoples and their gradual chrystallisation into independent nation states (like their independent Black neighbours in Lesotho, Botswana and Swaziland) will obviously demand an adjustment of the current geopolitical borders and boundaries of the Republic of South Africa. Once the process of emancipation has reached its conclusion, the Republic of South Africa will become a sovereign independent White nation state which will be associated with its Black neighbour states on the basis of political independence and economic interdependence.

Thus, there will emerge what is now referred to in officia
circles as a 'constellation of states', in each of which th
people will be free to preserve their own ways of life and deter
mine their own destinies. The Blacks having their own indepen
dent states, the question of their political rights withi
'White' South Africa no longer arises. Within the 'White' re
public, residential separation assists the Whites, Coloureds an
Asians to preserve their own group identities, including th
racial purity which is very highly valued by Afrikaners.

The official rationale for the policy of apartheid is chall
enged by those who view it as a faintly disguised strategy fo
racial domination. The geographical transfer of citizenship an
political rights (e.g. the franchise) from 'White' South Afric
to the 'homelands' for Blacks eliminates their numerica
supremacy in the 'White' Republic, leaving more Whites than th
other two groups (Coloureds and Asians) together. Instead o
emancipating the Blacks and giving them true independence
apartheid, separate development or multi-nationalism simply keep
them in a position of peripheral subordination to the Whites
The allocation of the Blacks to ten separate 'homelands' i
interpreted as a plan for divide and rule, rather than as a mean
of preserving tribal integrity.

Some evidence in support of this view is provided by the 197
'homeland' consolidation proposals (see Figure 1.1, page 12
which the government is still in the process of implementing
Not only are there ten 'homelands', but most of them comprise
number of separate blocks of land. KwaZulu, the most populous
is highly fragmented today and will still have ten block
separated by 'White' land if the consolidation plan is eve
completed. The 'independent republic' of Bophuthatswana has si
separate blocks, one of them (Thaba Nchu) almost 200 miles fro
its nearest neighbouring block. In addition to thi
'Balkanisation', the boundaries have been drawn so as to exclud
from the 'homelands' all industrial centres of any importance
most mineral resources, all but the smallest White settlements
and practically all transportation lines. The 'homelands' hav
no ports, and only limited access to the coasts. In short, it i
difficult to see these areas, even after consolidation, a
providing a satisfactory territorial basis for economicall
viable and truly independent nation states. Some of them, mos
notably KwaZulu, have in fact refused to consider 'independence
under the existing land allocation proposals.

Further evidence in favour of the racial domination inter
pretation is provided by population figures. Table 4.1 distin
guishes between the **de facto** and **de jure** populations of th
'homelands'. The de facto population refers to those actuall
there, the **de jure** to the tribal population allocated to th
homeland' in question. The de jure 'homeland' population (b) i
less than the **de facto** population (a) by the number of people o
other tribal groups in the 'homeland' in question. This i
generally fairly small but exceeds 400,000 in the case o
Bophuthatswana (ie one-third of the actual population are non
Tswana) and it is almost 300,000 for Lebowa. More significant
however, is the difference between the **de jure** population in th
appropriate 'homelands' (b) and the total for that tribal grou

(c). The final column of the table shows that the proportion of the tribal total actually resident in their 'homeland' varies from about 60 per cent in the case of three of the four 'independent republics' (listed first) down to as low as 16 per cent of the South African Swazi living in KaNgwane and 11 per cent of the Sotho for the Qwaqwa. Of the total of about 20 million Blacks, just less than half actually lived in their allotted 'homeland'. 1985 figures show 21.2 million Blacks or Africans, with 12.8 million in the 'homelands' leaving 8.4 million in 'White' South Africa. This figure, along with those living in the wrong 'homeland', is an indication of the discrepancy between the theory of tribal 'homelands' or 'Black states' and the reality of the actual population distribution.

Table 4.1   'Homeland' populations (1000), **de facto** and **de jure**

'Homeland' (tribe)	De facto (actual) population		De jure (tribal) population 1980		(b) as % of (c)
	1985	1980(a)	'Homeland' (b)	Total (c)	
Bophuthatswana (Tswana)	1,627	1,286	867	2,083	42
Ciskei (Xhosa)	925	630	628	1,072	59
Transkei (Xhosa)	2,947	2,622	2,492	4,157	60
Venda (Vhavenda)	455	343	328	522	63
Gazankulu (Tsonga)	495	477	381	985	39
KaNgwane (Swazi)	389	160	119	737	16
Kwa Ndebele (Ndebele)	233	166	134	679	20
KwaZulu (Zulu)	3,737	3,178	3,111	5,495	57
Lebowa (North Sotho)	1,842	1,658	1,363	2,350	58
Qwaqwa (South Sotho)	183	232	216	1,938	11
Total	12,833	10,752	9,639	20,018	48

Source: Population Census 1980 (SAIRR, 1982, 288), and 1985 (SAIRR, 1986, p. 1), preliminary results.

Note: All African population figures from the Census are subject to error, generally an under-enumeration. Some of the changes in **de facto** population between 1980 and 1985 arise from population relocation and boundary adjustments. De **jure** figures for 1985 are not available.

Within the cities, the racial domination interpretatio
emphasises the fact that the implementation of the Group Area Ac
has generally been to the advantage of the Whites. They hav
gained some attractive and conveniently located residential area
from the Coloureds and Indians, who have been forced into peri
pheral areas (see Figures 3.2 and 3.3 on pages 27 and 29) wher
they pose less competition or threat to control of the inne
city. There is an analogy here with the assignment of the Black
to peripheral locations nationally: the detached tribal 'home
land' blocks fragment what would otherwise be a continuou
crescent of Black territory threatening the economic heartland o
the Witwatersrand centred on Johannesburg.

The racial domination interpretation, like simplistic criti
ques stressing discrimination, tends to portray apartheid i
exclusively racial terms. They resemble the official rationale
with its emphasis on racial integrity and the elimination o
racial conflict. However, there is another interpretation, whic
sees racial domination as part of a broader system which has a
economic purpose: that of ensuring the continued production an
exploitation of cheap (Black) labour. This interpretation als
argues that, although racial conflict is an important element i
South Africa, an exclusively racial interpretation of aparthei
obscures the class cleavages which are present in any capitalis
society and which can to some extent transcend race.

There are two important ways in which the policy of aparthei
reduces the cost of labour in South Africa. First the 'home
lands' help to diffuse Black political power, thus damping dow
pressure for higher wages, better working conditions, fring
benefits and social services, which can be exerted by an organ
ised and united working class. The stress on racial and triba
affiliation under apartheid helps to prevent a broader working
class consciousness from developing. All discriminatory legis
lation whereby other races are paid less than Whites, certai
jobs are reserved for Whites, and trade union activities on th
part of Blacks are restricted, use racial identity to keep dow
the cost of certain people's labour.

The second way in which labour costs are depressed is tha
the 'homelands' enable some of these costs to be externalised, i
a literal geographical sense, as far as 'White' South Africa i
concerned, because they are borne within the 'homelands' or eve
outside South Africa itself. This strategy is used to particula
effect with the migrant labour on which the mines have tradition
ally relied (see Chapter 6). All the employers need pay for th
migrant worker is the cost of keeping the individual alive, fi
and reasonably content during the time of his contract; wage
little above subsistence are enough to attract workers. Migran
workers remit or bring back money to the 'homeland' for th
support of their families but this is supplemented from the loca
agricultural sector. When at home 'resting' or unemployed be
tween contracts, migrants are entitled to support from the loca
economy. Thus part of the full cost of maintaining a migran
labour system is, in effect, transferred to the area of origin
the 'homelands' or states bordering South Africa. Some of th
costs associated with what is, in effect, a permanent Blac
workforce in 'White' South Africa are also externalised throug

the requirement that certain social services be provided in the 'homelands' for their citizens in the 'White' Republic. Where Black dormitory towns on the edge of 'White' cities are defined as part of a 'homeland', Blacks working in 'White' South Africa have their social welfare costs met in the 'homeland'. The 'independence' of the 'homelands' makes it easier for the South African government to argue that the social support of those who live there is the responsibility of the governments of those black 'states' or 'republics' and not that of 'White' South Africa, even if large numbers of their 'citizens' actually work in the 'White' city. Thus 'White' South Africa avoids part of the full cost of the labour which it needs, and business profits accordingly.

Figure 4.1 summarises the main features of the spatial structure of exploitation in South Africa. The country is portrayed as a simple core/periphery dichotomy, the core representing the city and the periphery the Black/African 'homelands'. The periphery provides cheap labour (some of which also comes from other countries in southern Africa) and acts as a repository for surplus labour as well as for the transfer of political power from the core. Profits are generated and capital accumulated in the city, from the exploitation of cheap labour. A process of income redistribution in the core is suggested, whereby the product of

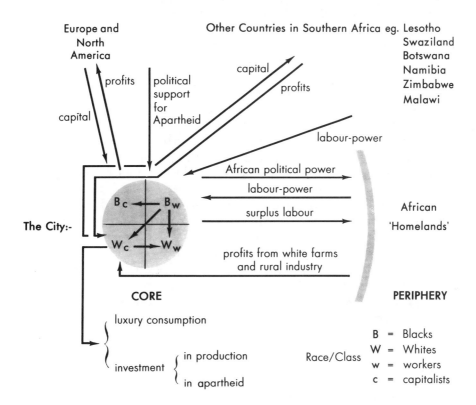

Figure 4.1 The spatial structure of exploitation in South Africa
     Source: Smith (1977, p. 262)

Black labour benefits White capital (promoting luxury consumption, investment in new productive capacity and expenditure required to maintain apartheid). The White working class gain from protected employment and the artificial maintenance of high living standards, and a small Black capitalist class themselves gain from the availability of cheap labour. Profits made in South Africa by multinational corporations are repatriated to Europe and North America, in return for which comes political support for the South African Government. Some capital generated in South Africa is also invested elsewhere in the sub-continent, as adjoining or nearby states which might otherwise be hostile (e.g. Zimbabwe) become tied to South Africa by economic dependence.

The above discussion outlines an interpretation of apartheid which stresses the economic foundations of political practice in South Africa. It incorporates something of the racial domination perspective, setting this in a broader context. While stressing that apartheid and capitalism in South Africa are mutually supportive, it does recognise some contradictions between them. For example, racial domination reduces the mobility of Black labour and impedes its efficient utilisation; low Black wages limit purchasing power; and the cost of maintaining apartheid affects White living standards (including RSA subsidy of 'homeland' budgets). However, a fuller exposition and evaluation of the argument requires more details concerning South Africa's economy and employment practices, along with an account of certain aspects of contemporary urbanisation and planning. This is dealt with in the next four chapters.

Before proceeding, however, it is necessary to recognise certain respects in which the contemporary interpretation of apartheid is changing. Soon after his election as Prime Minister in 1978, P. W. Botha was telling the Whites that they must 'adapt or die' and that 'apartheid is a recipe for permanent conflict'. More recently, apartheid itself has officially been declared dead (see Chapter 10). However, this does not mean that the basic principle of racial separation has been abandoned - far from it. There has certainly been some relaxation of petty apartheid, and constitutional 'reforms' represent a retreat from total White monopoly of political power. But the basic policy of 'independent homelands' and residential segregation in 'White' South Africa remains intact in early 1987, despite suggestions that even some senior Nationalists are prepared to consider a new political dispensation for Blacks and relaxation of 'group areas'.

The withdrawal of some large (mainly American) firms from South Africa in the mid-1980s calls into question the extent to which the White government and the international capital continue to share common interests. Capital is concerned about the Nationalists' capacity to maintain the social stability on which reliable profit-making depends, and has also to consider image problems arising from association with apartheid. If social control can be restored, and White domination conveyed in more acceptable terms via 'reforms', the support of international capital may well be regained - as long as Black labour remains cheap.

5 The economy

Plate 12   Central Johannesburg - the 'City of Gold' on the
           Witwatersrand in the major economic heartland of
           'White' South Africa.

Plate 13   A Zulu kraal or homestead of traditional form accom-
           modating a family group, in KwaZulu - one of the 'home-
           lands' or 'Black national states'.

5 THE ECONOMY

The development of an advanced industrial economy in South Africa was closely associated with the exploitation of minerals, most spectacularly gold and diamonds. The country's mineral wealth is extensive and varied, and includes material of great strategic importance as well as essential elements in modern manufacturing. However, minerals are far less important in the economy than they were. Table 5.1 summarises changes in the sectoral origin of GDP since 1911, revealing the growing importance of manufacturing and related services.

Table 5.1 Sectoral origin of gross domestic product (%)

Sector	1911	1939	1983
Gold mining	18.7	16.3	10.4
Other mining	8.9	2.0	4.7
Agriculture, forestry and fishing	21.1	13.6	4.7
Manufacturing, construction, electricity gas, water	5.5	16.6	32.0
Other services	45.8	51.5	48.2

Source: RSA (1985, p. 357)

Table 5.2 summarises the employment structure of the RSA (i.e. excluding Transkei, Bophuthatswana, Venda and Ciskie) by race groups. The addition of the TBVC area gives a total of 10.84 million economically active, of whom 68 per cent are Blacks. Blacks dominate mining and account for just over half manufacturing employment in the RSA. Of the 9,758,000 economically active in the RSA in 1985, almost 5 million were reported to be in agriculture and domestic service. However, figures for these activities are hard to establish as the conditions under which Blacks are employed by farmers and households are often casual, and traditional agricultural practices in the 'homelands' make it difficult to define who is actually 'economically active'. Earnings in agriculture and domestic service are in any event generally much lower than in other sectors; the large number of people involved helps to explain low living standards among the mass of the Black population.

The economy of South Africa is highly polarised geographically. In the early stages, economic activity was concentrated in the coastal enclaves of Cape Town and, later, Durban, after the typical pattern of colonial development. The discovery of gold shifted the economic centre of gravity inland, to the Witwatersrand, the supremacy of which was consolidated by industrialisation.

Table 5.2 Employment structure by race (1000s)

	Blacks	Whites	Coloureds	Asians	Total
Economically active population 1985	6,308	2,110	1042	298	9,758
Effectively active in TBVC 1985	1,083	n	n	n	1,083
Employment in mining 1985	637	78	9	1	725
Employment in manufacturing 1984	681	299	234	87	1,301

Source: Official government sources, from SAIRR (1986, p. 133, 157-60, pp. 164); n = negligible

The present spatial structure of the economy is shown i Figure 5.1. The pattern is dominated by the principal metro politan region centred on Johannesburg - usually referred to a the PWV region (Pretoria, Witwatersrand, Vereeniging). This i part of a wider area of relatively intensive economic activit which extends along the main communications corridor to Durban o the Natal coast. Other areas of relatively intensive developmen (the 'inner periphery') correspond with the inland cities o Kimberley and Bloemfontein and extend along much of the sout coast. Areas of less intensive activity (the 'intermediat periphery') come next, then the 'outer periphery' of largel agricultural areas. The 'homelands' form part of this oute periphery, ringing the economic heartland centred on the PW region.

Almost 70 per cent of South Africa's GDP is generated in th eight main metropolitan centres. The PWV region alone account for 40 per cent. The rest of 'White' South Africa generate about 30 per cent. The 'homelands' (including the 'independen republics') account for only about 3 per cent of GDP. Thes figures are in sharp contrast to the distribution of populatior which divides roughly into one-third in the major metropolita centres, one third in the rest of 'White' South Africa and one third in the 'homelands'.

Foreign investment in South Africa is an important currer issue. Capital from overseas is attracted by cheap labour an relatively high profits, and multi-national concerns are some times accused of supporting apartheid (though they can also exer cise a beneficial influence on employment practices). Foreigr controlled manufacturing activity involves about 1300 firm employing 400,000 or so workers. Almost 60 per cent of th employment is accounted for by firms from the UK and 25 per cer by American firms. At the beginning of 1987 Britain accounte for about 45 per cent of foreign investment in South Africa valued at £6,000 million, compared with America's £900 million.

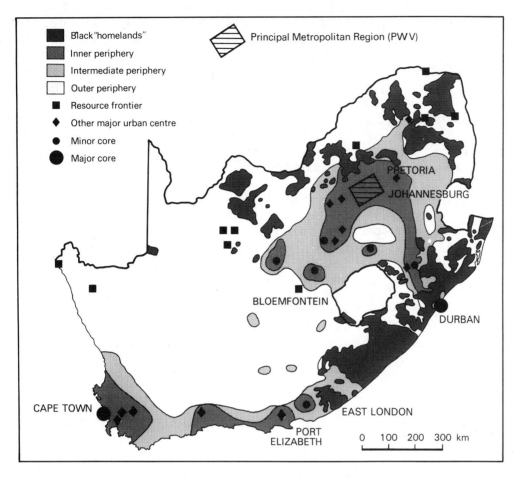

Legend:

- Black "homelands"
- Inner periphery
- Intermediate periphery
- Outer periphery
- ■ Resource frontier
- ♦ Other major urban centre
- ● Minor core
- ⬤ Major core
- Principal Metropolitan Region (PWV)

PRETORIA
JOHANNESBURG
BLOEMFONTEIN
DURBAN
EAST LONDON
PORT ELIZABETH
CAPE TOWN

0   100 200 300 km

re 5.1   The spatial structure of the South African economy
Source: Based on Fair (1982, p. 51) after J. Browett

The external orientation of the South African economy is a
ce of vulnerability as well as strength. Opposition to
theid from overseas is increasingly being expressed in dis-
stment or withdrawal of firms from South Africa, and in
omic sanctions which include restrictions on trade. America
taken the lead: during the past decade, measures enacted by
es, cities and other local authorities in the United States
involved a total of $5 billion in disinvestment from United
es corporations and banks involved in South Africa. The
htened unrest within South Africa since September 1984 has
ed to precipitate the withdrawal of such well-known firms as
ral Motors, Honeywell, Kodak and Revlon, culminating in the
t major British departure with the sale of the South African
ts of Barclays Bank in November 1986. The United States, the
and other countries have imposed various economic sanctions.
e measures have exacerbated a recession in the South African
omy, resulting in slow (or no) growth, rising unemployment,
a dramatic decline in the value of the Rand.

Externally induced economic pressure certainly hurts South
cans (including Blacks who depend on foreign investment and
e for their jobs). But the outside world in general and the
tern' capitalist world in particular still depends on South
ca for crucial minerals, and this acts as a constraint on

American and European sanctions. For example, the United Stat
relies heavily on imports from South Africa and its neighbou
for manganese, chromium, cobalt and the platinum group of mine
als, all of which are critical to military operations. Table 5
shows South Africa's contribution to production and reserves
major minerals for which the country is ranked first or second
output within the 'western' world. Conspicuous by its absence
oil. South Africa's lack of a domestic source of oil is a maj
weakness in the face of threats of sanctions – hence the strat
gic significance of the Sasol plant which produce oil from t
plentiful national coal resources.

Gold remains vitally important to the South African econom
making it highly sensitive to volatile international markets.
rise in the price of gold stimulates the economy, by encouragi
investment in the gold-mining industry and through the multipli
effect on other activities; a fall in price can induce
exacerbate recession, as in the early 1980s. The role of gold
the international monetary system is a further element in t
strategic importance of South Africa, giving the capitalist wor
a strong vested interest in both the political stability of t
country and perpetuation of the cheap labour on which the l
cost production of gold depends.

Table 5.3   South Africa's role in selected mineral production a
            reserves

	Production 1981 (%)		Reserves 1982 (%	
	"West"	World	"West"	World
Gold	69	49	63	50
Vanadium	60	42	61	37
Alumino-silicates	49	42	47	38
Chrome ore	43	28	58	57
Manganese ore	40	21	93	80
Platinum group metals	40	22	83	70
Vermicilite	39	35	29	28
Diamonds	33	23	29	27
Antimony	27	18	17	7
Zirconium minerals	19	17	19	17
Fluorspar	16	10	46	34
Coal	9	5	18	10

Source: RSA (1985, pp. 564-5)

Note: The 'west' is the world excluding Comecon (USSR a
        Eastern Europe), Afghanistan, Albania, China, Nor
        Korea and Yugoslavia.

Figure 5.2 illustrates the importance of minerals in South Africa's exports. The pattern of exports excluding gold emphasises links with Western Europe, which also accounts for about 40 per cent of South Africa's imports.

South Africa's economic relations with neighbouring countries is a further aspect of external interdependence with important strategic considerations. Malawi, Mozambique and Zimbabwe as well as Botswana, Lesotho and Swaziland all have South Africa as their main trading nation. All have large numbers of their citizens working in South Africa as migrants (see Table 6.3, page 54), and gain substantially from their remittances. Botswana, Lesotho and Swaziland all have well over half their tourists from South Africa. South Africa also supplies crucial materials, including oil and electricity, and acts as a conduit for exports - especially from Botswana, Lesotho and Zimbabwe. These links help to protect South Africa from what might otherwise be more vigorous antagonism from the so-called 'front line' states.

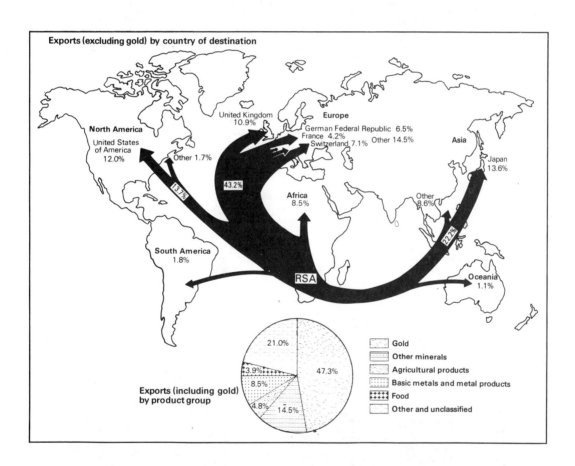

Figure 5.2   Sectoral origin of South Africa's exports, and desti-
             nation of exports excluding gold, average 1980-84
             **Source: The Debt Standstill and Beyond, Focus on Key
             Economic Issues** No. 38, Merbank, 1985

48

Plate 14   Part of Soweto, the vaste, sprawling township housing
over a million Black residents in the Johannesburg
metropolitan area. It was here that serious riots took
place in 1976.

Plate 15   Hostels for Black workers in one of the townships of
Cape Town. It is in such accommodation that increasing
numbers of single workers are expected to live as the
settlement of Black families in 'White' South Africa is
discouraged.

6 Labour supply and demand

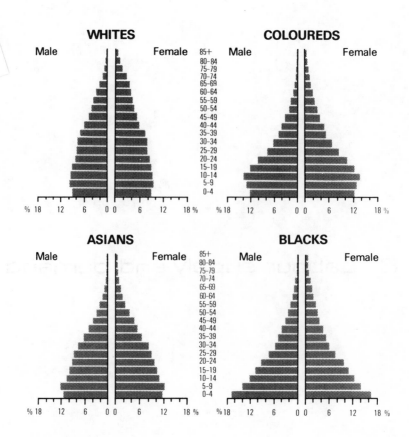

Figure 6.1   Age structure of the population by race group 1980
          Source: RSA (1983, p. 31)

Table 6.1   Population trends by race group

	Blacks	Whites	Coloureds	Asians	Tota
Increase 1970-85 (1000s)	5,857	868	803	172	7,65
Increase 1970-85 (%)	37.7	21.7	39.2	27.3	35.
Projected population in year 2000	34,900	5,300	3,700	1,100	45,00
Projected increase 1985-2000	13,307	709	846	298	15,16
Births/1000 popn 1980	39.1	16.5	27.8	24.4	
Deaths/1000 popn 1980	11.0	8.3	9.2	5.9	
Natural increase 1980	28.1	8.2	18.6	18.1	

Source: Increase 1970-85 from Table 1.1; projection for 2000 by L
          Sadie from SAIRR (1982, p. 52); other figures from RSA
          (1985, p. 27)

Note: Table 7.5 contains population projections beyond 2000

6 LABOUR SUPPLY AND DEMAND

The relationship between labour supply and demand is crucial to an understanding of apartheid. Taking South Africa as a whole, the supply of labour greatly exceeds the demand generated by the modern sectors of the economy, and control of supply is a crucial feature of government policy. This control means, in effect, restricting access by Blacks to 'White' areas in general, and the core (cities) in particular, to numbers consistent with employment opportunities, keeping the rest of the Black population in their peripheral 'homelands'.

At the heart of the 'over-supply' of labour is the rate of increase of the Black population. Table 6.1 shows that this was almost twice as high for Blacks as for Whites between 1970 and 1985. The Black population rose by over 5.8 million, the rest of the population by 1.8 million. The high natural increase among Blacks is accounted for almost entirely by the high birth rate. Population pyramids (Figure 6.1) show 54.6 per cent of Blacks in the age group 0-19 compared with 39.7 per cent of the Whites. More Coloureds are in this age group (55.5 per cent) than Asians (50.5) and the Coloureds have a higher birth rate, but the difference in natural increase is narrowed by the low death rate among Asians. Population projections for the year 2000 show a massive increase in the number of Blacks, especially when compared to that of the Whites. Blacks will comprise 77.6 per cent of South Africa's total population compared with 72.0 per cent in 1985, while the proportion White will fall from 15.6 per cent to 11.8 in 2000.

The relationship between Black population and employment prospects in South Africa is a matter of concern. Official figures put the number of Blacks unemployed in the RSA at about 600,000 in late 1986, or 10 per cent of those economically active. However, other sources suggest that unemployment is actually much higher - anything up to 3.5 million and a million in the cities alone. There are an additional 350,000 Blacks seeking work each year, compared with an average of roughly 120,000 new jobs annually since 1970. Recent estimates suggest that unemployment could reach 5 million by the year 2000. And to add to the problem, the current recession and withdrawal of some overseas firms makes it hard for the present inadequate level of job creation to be maintained. Thus there is every reason to expect the present substantial shortfall of demand for labour in relation to supply to grow to enormous proportions over the next decade or two.

This mismatch between labour supply and demand is selective in two important respects. First, it is racially selective, with disproportionate impact on the rapidly growing Black population, most of which lacks the skills and education to compete for limited employment opportunities. Secondly, it is geographically selective, concentrated in the 'homelands' and in the Black townships of the 'White' cities.

The actual organisation of labour supply may now be examined in more detail. Black labour employed in 'White' South Africa

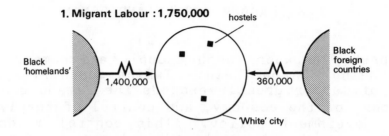

1. Migrant Labour : 1,750,000

hostels

Black 'homelands'

1,400,000

360,000

Black foreign countries

'White' city

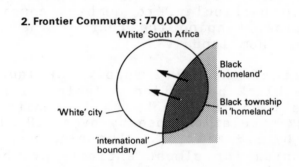

2. Frontier Commuters : 770,000

'White' South Africa

Black 'homeland'

Black township in 'homeland'

'White' city

'international' boundary

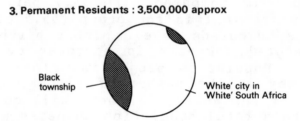

3. Permanent Residents : 3,500,000 approx

Black township

'White' city in 'White' South Africa

Figure 6.2   Different spatial forms of Black labour in South
           Africa
           Source: Approximate figures from Tables 6.2, 6.3 and
           6.4

may be divided into three categories: (1) migrant workers (2)
so-called frontier commuters and (3) those who are in effect
permanent residents of 'White' South Africa (Figure 6.2).   It is
government policy to keep the third category as small as possible
and to encourage the maintenance and further development of the
other two.

The migrant labour system has a long history in South Africa.
The traditional pattern, still largely adhered to today, is for
the worker to live in a compound or dormitory at the mine or
other place of employment, returning home after completion of his
contract (usually of one year's duration) only to leave again
shortly for a further contract.   The system now involves many
workers in manufacturing industry, and this pattern of oscilla-
tion between single existence in the 'White' city and brief
spells of family life in the 'homeland' or foreign country is
familiar to Blacks all over southern Africa.

In 1982/3 there were about 1.75 million Black migrant workers
in 'White' South Africa.   Most of them came from the 'homelands'
(Table 6.2):   the number has increased by about 450,000 since
1970, and now accounts for about one third of the total labour
force of the 'homelands'.   The spatial pattern of origin has
remained much the same over the decade covered by the table,
except for a substantial absolute increase in the number from the

Table 6.2   Migrant labour from 'homelands' to 'White' South
            Africa

'Homeland' of origin	1970	1977	1982
Bophuthatswana	150,000	179,000	236,000
Ciskei	52,000	47,000	59,000
Transkei	268,000	263,000	346,000
Venda	22,000	26,000	37,000
Gazankulu	40,000	39,000	64,000
KaNgwane	18,000	29,000	67,000
KwaNdebele	11,000	24,000	52,000
KwaZulu	270,000	305,000	294,000
Lebowa	140,000	140,000	180,000
Qwaqwa	4,000	43,000	60,000
Total	975,000	1095,000	1395,000

Source: 1970, 1977: RSA (198?, p. 249); 1982: SAIRR (1985, p.
          258) - from original ficial sources

Transkei and large relative increases in some 'homelands' which
were previously very small suppliers of migrant labour - notably
Qwaqwa, Kwadebele and KaNgwane.

     As the 'homeland' supply of migrant workers has increased, so
foreign supply has fallen (Table 6.3). The number of Blacks from
foreign countries rose to a peak of 836,000 in 1960, and then
declined during the period of decolonisation in southern Africa.
The mines illustrate how the balance has shifted: in 1964 Blacks
from foreign countries accounted for just over 60 per cent of the
total labour force of the mines but figures for 1985 for Africans
employed in gold, platinum and copper mines which were members of
the Chamber of Mines show 257,887 of 472,467 coming from the
'homelands', leaving about 47 per cent from foreign sources.
While some of the loss can be related to political events, e.g.
in Mozambique, the most dramatic reduction was from Malawi
following an air crash in 1974 in which a large number of Malawi
migrants were killed and which led to the suspension of
recruitment.

     The second category of Black labour is that of the commuter.
This term has a special meaning in South Africa: commuters are
defined as Blacks who reside in the 'homelands' but travel daily
to work in the cities, industrial districts or rural areas of
'White' South Africa. In apartheid theory, they thus commute
across what is now (in the case of 'independent republics') or

what will eventually be (in the case of the remaining 'national states') an international boundary. For this reason the term 'frontier commuter' is sometimes adopted, to distinguish them from conventional commuters. Their special significance is that, whereas the migrant labour system has a long history and exists elsewhere in the world, the 'frontier commuter' is a creation of apartheid and has meaning only within the objectives of South African government policy.

Table 6.3 Migrant labour from foreign countries

Country of origin	1973	1977	1983
Angola	42	8 05	68
Botswana	46,192	43,159	29,967
Lesotho	148,856	160,634	145,797
Malawi	139,714	12,761	29,622
Mozambique	127,198	111,257	61,218
Swaziland	10,032	20,750	16,773
Zambia	684	766	743
Zimbabwe	3,250	32,716	7,742
Total (inc. others)	485,100	391,484	358,035

Source: 1973, 1977: A. Lemon, in Smith (1982, p. 69); 1983: RSA (1985, p. 220) - from original official sources

Note: The 1983 total is inflated by inclusion of Namibia for the first time among 'others'; the total without 'others' is 277,930 in 1983 compared with 475,968 in 1973.

     The beginning of 'frontier commuting' as an explicit element in apartheid planning strategy was associated with an important change in policy over Black townships. In 1967 local authorities were required to obtain central government approval before initiating any new Black housing schemes, the intention being to prevent further townships being set up in 'White' South Africa if they could be established in a conveniently situated part of a 'homeland'. From 1968 Blacks were allowed only to rent houses in townships in 'White' South Africa, whereas in the 'homeland' they could buy, thus encouraging Blacks to move to 'homeland' townships. The 'homeland' locations help the South African government to legitimise the disenfranchising of Black residents and assist the externalisation of costs of social welfare support.

Table 6.4 shows the enormous increase in 'frontier commuting' during the 1970s, especially the first half of the decade. The pre-eminence of Bophuthatswana and KwaZulu reflects the proximity of parts of these 'homelands' to cities in 'White' South Africa. The largest commuter flows are from Bophuthatswana into Pretoria and from KwaZulu into Durban.

Table 6.4 Commuters from 'homelands' to 'White' South Africa

'Homeland' of origin	1970	1976	1982
Bophuthatswana	84,000	154,900	173,000
Ciskei	40,000	36,900	38,000
Transkei	3,400	7,100	8,000
Venda	3,000	3,700	6,000
Gazankulu	3,400	7,800	9,000
KaNgwane	3,000	23,000	44,000
KwaNdebele	---	---	12,000
KwaZulu	127,000	325,000	395,000
Lebowa	26,000	46,300	76,000
Qwaqwa	1,000	1,800	12,000
Total	290,800	606,500	773,000

Source: Bureau for Economic Development, Cooperation and Research. 1970 and 1976 courtesy A. Lemon; 1983: SAIRR (1985, pp. 258-9)

The third category of Black worker lives, in effect, permanently in 'White' South Africa. In apartheid terminology, they are 'permanently absent' from their 'homeland'. Official figures for 1980 place their number at almost exactly 3 million, but the subsequent increase plus an allowance for under-enumeration suggests something more like 3.5 million Black `workers live permanently in 'White' South Africa. These are the inhabitants of the townships which are not in the 'homelands', and of the rural areas of 'White' South Africa. They are the major inconsistency in the concept of a 'White' Republic, for their presence is necessary to the functioning of the economy. While they may be portrayed as citizens of some 'homeland', links may be tenuous at best: most Blacks living in 'White' areas have been born there, and have neither children nor parents living in a 'homeland'. The South African government is now recognising that any residual 'White' Republic of South Africa will have a large, permanent Black population.

It is in the major economic heartland of the PWV that this inconsistency is revealed most clearly. Figure 6.3 (page 57) shows the three cities of Pretoria, Johannesburg and Vereeniging and highlights the position of the major Black townships. While Pretoria has its own townships of Atteridgeville and Mamelodi inherited from the pre-1967 era, it is close enough to part of Bophuthatswana to take advantage of frontier commuting. Large townships have been built within Bophuthatswana; they are in fact displaced dormitories for Black workers employed in Pretoria. Their inhabitants, as Bophuthatswana citizens, have the vote in the 'Republic' of Bophuthatswana.

The Witwatersrand, however, is too far from Bophuthatswana or any other 'homeland' to take advantage of large-scale frontier commuting. The Black labour not provided by migrants must therefore have places of residence in 'White' territory; hence the existence of massive townships here, and at Vereeniging. The largest of the townships is Soweto. The actual population of Soweto exceeds 1.5 million, its official population being swelled by a few hundred thousand illegal residents. About 250,000 people travel into Johannesburg daily, on 100 trains. Major programmes to improve living conditions have been initiated since the 1976 riots, including bringing electricity into over 100,000 houses. However, facilities remain very limited indeed for a city of this size, and there are high rates of crime against persons and property to add to the pervading poverty, social deprivation and environmental degradation.

This discussion should have helped further to clarify the role of the 'homelands' in the grand design of apartheid. Applying a one-third activity rate to the de facto 'homeland' population of 13.8 million Blacks gives about 4.25 million economically active. Tables 6.2 and 6.3 show that almost 2.2 million are accounted for by migrant workers and frontier commuters, and to this should be added a considerable number of people illegally going to 'White' South Africa to work as migrants or commuters. Whatever the true figure, it is clear that a majority of the working population of the 'homelands' is employed in 'White' South Africa.

The degree of economic dependence of the 'homelands' on those who work in 'White' South Africa is illustrated by figures compiled by the government's Department of Statistics for 1980, for the six 'national states' (i.e. excluding the TBVC area). The sum of income from migrant workers and frontier commuters is over 3 times the income from 'homeland' domestic sources (GDP), and represents almost 80 per cent of Gross National Income. GNI per capita for these 'homelands' together would fall from R488 to little more than R10 without income from external resources; their combined Gross Domestic product (GDP) in 1980 was R128 per capita. The so-called "independent republics" also rely heavily on income from their residents working in the RSA. Some 'homelands' are less dependent than others: Bophuthatswana's GDP accounts for about half GNI, whereas in KwaZulu it is less than a quarter. The relative importance of 'frontier commuters' and migrants varies considerably, from Bophuthatswana's high commuter income, through KwaZulu where both are very important, to the Transkei's extreme reliance on migrants. Most domestically

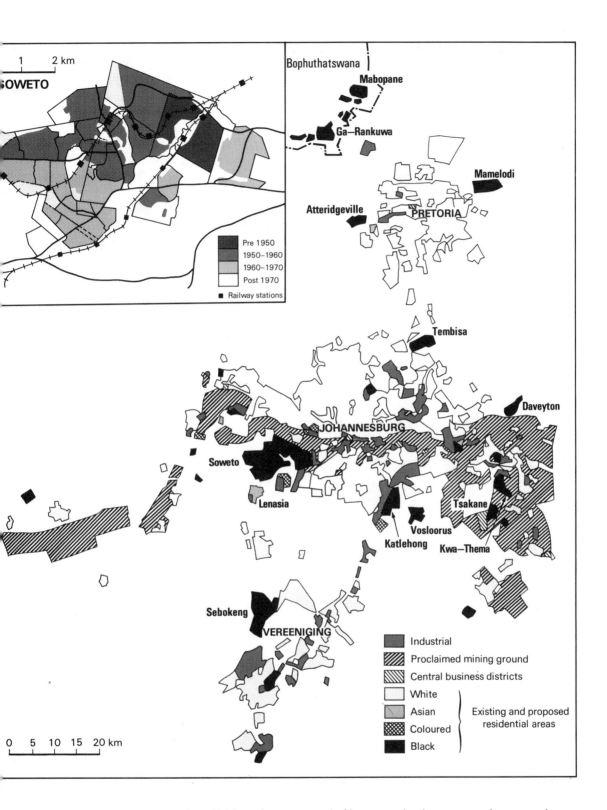

Figure 6.3   The Pretoria-Witwatersrand-Vereeniging region, show-
ing the location of major Black townships
Source: Southern Transvaal Land Use Map, Urban and
Regional Research Unit, University of the
Witwatersrand

generated 'homeland' income comes from agriculture and withou
the external sources poverty would be universal and extreme. Th
migrant and commuter incomes themselves are deceptive whe
attributed to the 'homelands', for a substantial proportion ar
spent where they are earned - in 'White' South Africa.

The dependency relationship between 'homelands' and 'White
South Africa is not entirely one-way. The funds allocated by th
South African government in what it describes as 'developmen
aid' to the Black 'national states' was about R2500 million i
1985/86, with a further R1000 million or so going to the fou
'independent' homelands. This is some measure of the price pai
by the RSA for what is to the Republic (though not to the 'home
lands') a self-imposed dependency whereby the role of the 'home
lands' in the emerging spatial organisation of labour supply i
maintained.

7 Urbanisation

Plate 16   Crossroads, the Black spontaneous settlement on the
            edge of Cape Town.   Over 3 million South Africans now
            live in conditions like this.

Plate 17   Interior of a 'shack' in Crossroads.   Such settlements
            provide the opportunity for family life for men whose
            wives are not legally entitled to be in the 'White'
            city.

7 URBANISATION

By the beginning of the present century there were 350,000 Blacks in urban areas in South Africa. As numbers grew so did the shanty-town slums on the edge of South Africa's towns and cities. Slum clearance and township construction brought the system under some degree of order, while the introduction of formal measures of influx control kept inward migration to manageable numbers. Recently, however, there have been important new developments, including the urbanisation of the 'homelands' associated with 'frontier commuting' and certain features of Third-World urbanisation reasserting themselves in a way which presently defies the authorities' power totally to control the formation of South Africa's cities. Urbanisation in South Africa is thus both a product of apartheid and a challenge to its future.

Table 7.1 shows the increasing urbanisation of the population of each race group. The proportion of Whites and Asians/Indians in urban areas by 1980 resembled that of the population of the advanced industrial nations of the world. The Coloured figure is also high. The most significant feature, however, is the rapid increase in the proportion of the Black/African population in urban areas.

The polarised space-economy of South Africa is reflected in a marked concentration of its urban population. Table 7.2 shows the proportion of the total population of each race group in 'White' South Africa living in the four largest metropolitan areas, which together accounted for 53.4 per cent of 'White' South Africa's total population in 1980 (49.9 per cent in 1970). The pattern is dominated by the PWV area, with 30 per cent of all the Whites and 33 per cent of the Blacks. The Black figure, high when compared with the other metropolitan areas, especially Durban, is explained by the fact that most of its Black labour force is in 'White' South Africa (as explained in Chapter 6) and not in townships in adjoining 'homelands'. In Cape Town the Black population has been kept down by the existence of a 'Coloured Labour Preference Areas' covering most of Cape Province and designed to give the Coloureds protection in the labour market from Black competition. About 43 per cent of all Blacks in 'White' South Africa live in the four major metropolitan areas, and when other cities and towns are added well over half the Blacks are in urban areas. About 31 per cent of the RSA's Black population now live in urban areas in 'White' South Africa.

Government policy with respect to Blacks in urban areas within 'White' South Africa has changed significantly in recent years. In 1977 Blacks were given some control over local affairs pertaining to their own communities, through elected councils. In 1978 a 99-year leasehold system was introduced to encourage Blacks to buy their own homes, and this was subsequently extended to freehold. Low earnings limit demand, but prices of township houses well below market value have been ued to entice Blacks of

modest means into private ownership. However, this developmen
is barely relevant to the mass of the Black population who canno
afford to buy, and for whom existing housing is usually overcrowded and of poor quality.

Table 7.1   Urban population by race group (% of total) 1904-
            1980

	Blacks	Whites	Coloureds	Asians
1904	10.4	53.6	49.2	36.4
1911	13.0	53.0	50.4	52.8
1921	14.0	59.7	52.4	60.4
1936	19.0	68.2	58.0	69.5
1946	24.3	75.6	62.7.	72.8
1951	27.9	79.1	66.2	77.6
1960	31.8	83.6	68.3	83.2
1970	33.0	86.7	74.3	86.2
1980	38.0	88.0	77.0	91.0

Source: RSA (1983, p. 32)

Table 7.2   Population in major metropolitan areas by race group
            (% of total in 'White' South Africa) 1980

Metropolitan area	Blacks	Whites	Coloureds	Asians	Total
Pretoria-Witwatersrand Vereeniging	33.01	41.33	7.03	12.35	30.32
Greater Cape Town	2.11	13.08	39.27	1.94	10.40
Durban-Pinetown- Pietermaritzburg	4.39	9.33	2.82	74.38	8.92
Port Elizabeth- Uitenhage	3.39	3.82	5.98	0.87	3.77

Source: RSA (1983, p. 35)

A major trend during the 1970s was what is generally referred to as the urbanisation of the 'homelands'. Table 7.3 shows a large increase in the number of housing units and population in 'proclaimed' (i.e. officially designated) towns in the 'homelands'. These figures suggest that almost 20 per cent of the 'homeland' population lives in urban areas, but the true figure now must be higher. Taking the 1.5 million formally classified as urban at the 1980 Census, adding an estimate of well over 4 million of the 'rural' population in what are effectively urban settlements near the metropolitan areas, and allowing for the rapidly expanding 'squatter' settlements (see page 64), suggests somewhat more than half the total population of almost 13 million in the 'homelands' living in conditions which could be considered urban.

Table 7.3   Population and housing in proclaimed towns in 'homelands' 1970-1981

| 'Homeland' | Housing units | | Population | | % of de facto popn. 1980 |
	1970	1981	1970	1981	
Bophuthatswana	18,866	39,743	126,095	224,331	16.5
Ciskei	15,960	28,437	111,444	244,699	35.7
Transkei			no data		
Venda	153	1,427	828	11,319	2.0
Gazankulu	843	2,896	4,932	15,742	3.1
KaNgwane	745	9,007	4,739	67,214	31.9
KwaNdebele	–	4,816	–	19,937	9.1
KwaZulu	31,934	88,321	200,694	738,117	20.7
Lebowa	10,701	18,715	77,037	131,551	7.1
QwaQwa	335	3,982	1,009	18,901	6.2

Source: 1970: RSA (1983, p. 247); 1981:   SAIRR (1983, pp, 439-40)

There are two main reasons for the rapid increase in the urban population of the 'homelands', both of which have been alluded to in earlier sections. The first is the implementation of the policy of resettling Blacks from 'White' rural and, more particularly, urban areas, by moving them into the 'homelands'. The second is the effective freezing of the construction of family housing for Blacks in 'White' areas as from the beginning of 1968, and the associated development of townships in the 'homelands' as dormitories for 'frontier commuters'. However, some of the increase is simply a result of boundary changes, e.g. the incorporation of Umlazi and KwaMashu into KwaZulu.

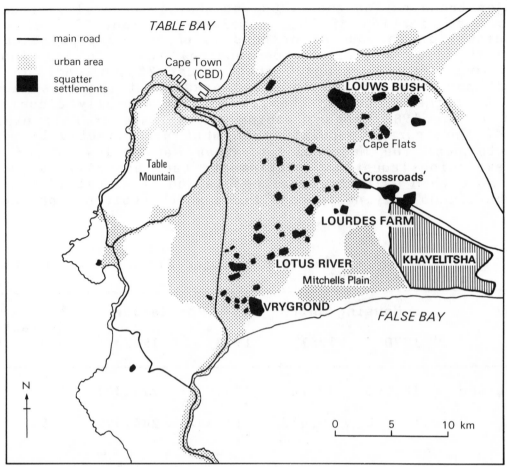

Figure 7.1   Areas of spontaneous settlement in the Western Cape
Source: Smith (1982, p. 33) based on Western (1981, p. 280), following Ellis et al (1977)

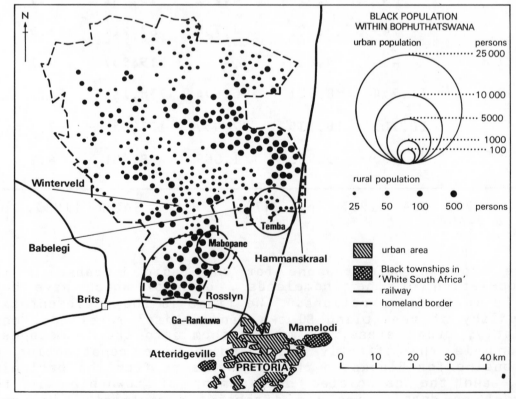

Figure 7.2   Population distribution in part of Bophuthatswana, north of Pretoria
Source: Smith (1982, p. 40); population distribution based on map by P. Smit

One of the most important features of contemporary urbanisation in South Africa is spontaneous or 'squatter' settlement,
which is a widespread phenomenon around cities throughout the
Third World. The number of people involved is hard to state
accurately but recent estimates suggest they number 1.25 million
of the 2 million Blacks in Greater Durban (including 500,000 in
Inanda), over 250,000 in Edendale-Zwartkops near Peitermaritzburg
and over 100,000 at Mdantsane in Ciskei, as well as hundreds of
thousands in the Western Cape and the Winterveld area of
Bophuthatswana (see page 67). Most of them are Blacks, but there
are also substantial numbers of Coloureds and some Indians
involved. The proportion of South Africa's Blacks living in
spontaneous settlements may now be approaching 20 per cent.

The essence of spontaneous settlement is that people occupy
land without authorisation, and construct their own homes out of
whatever material may be readily available. Spontaneous settlement can provide Blacks with greater personal freedom than they
have living in the townships or compounds of 'White' South
Africa, where the authorities can exercise such a high degree of
control. They enable Blacks who could not otherwise live in the
'White' cities to gain entry in circumstances where their pre-
sence is hard to detect. They also provide the opportunity for
family life for those men who are legally entitled to be in
'White' South Africa but whose wives have not qualified for
residence and hence for formal housing.

Two cases may be used to illustrate spontaneous settlement in
South Africa. The first is the Western Cape, where there are
large areas of spontaneous setlement in the Cape Town metropolitan area (Figure 7.1). Spontaneous settlements have been erected
by both Blacks and Coloureds. The former are unable or unwilling
to live in the formal townships or in hostels. The latter have
resorted to spontaneous settlement because of the shortage of
housing for Coloureds. Estimates of the population in spontaneous settlements at the end of the 1970s suggest figures of
180,000 Coloureds and 30,000 Blacks, out of a total population of
1.1 million in metropolitan Cape Town; today it could be a third
of a million.

The settlement known as Crossroads in the Western Cape has
become a **cause célèbre**, drawing international attention to spontaneous settlement in South Africa and to the government response. Crossroads is on the eastern edge of Cape Town (Figure
7.1) and adjoins the Black township of Nyanga. By the end of the
1970s it had a population of 20-25,000 living in over 3000 self-
constructed structures. Far from being a shiftless mass of
unemployed and illegal immigrants, crime-prone and a threat to
social order, which is how the government seeks to portray the
inhabitants of spontaneous settlements, those in Crossroads are
for the most part a stable element in the workforce, necessary to
the city economy. Indeed, such settlements are to the advantage
of white employers (industrial and domestic) as they enable part
of the 'homeland' labour reserve to be transferred to a location
convenient to the metropolitan labour market, yet lacking the
security and permanence of a formal township.

The attitude of the authorities to spontaneous settlement i 'White' South Africa has been largely negative, however. Man have been destroyed by the bulldozer and their inhabitant shipped off to a 'homeland'. Government figures show that b 1981 half the 50,000 or so 'huts' officially registered in 197 had been demolished, probably affecting over 100,000 people, an this applied only to Coloured and Asian settlements. Th demolition of spontaneous settlements and the removal of thei inhabitants has no doubt been pursued with even greater vigou with respect to Blacks, especially in 'White' South Africa. U to the end of 1986 South African newspapers carried frequen stories concerning the relocation of 'illegal shack dwellers'.

However, spontaneous settlement in general and the Crossroad cases in particular have stimulated a public debate in Sout Africa on the role of informal activity in housing the growin urban Black population. Interest was aroused in the so-calle site-and-service schemes which have been adopted in some Thir World countries, whereby the authorities provide land and utilit lines (water and electricity) and people are permitted t construct their own dewellings. Thus spontaneous settlement i transformed from a problem to a solution to housing needs, in th hands of the people but in locations chosen and controlled by th State. This is how the 'problem' of Crossroads is now bein tackled, but not without difficulty and conflict.

In 1982 the population of Crossroads was estimated to hav risen to 60,000. The settlement had survived by virtue of th publicity which its possible destruction attracted and throug the tenacity of its residents. In 1979 the Minister of Coopera- tion and Development (i.e. Black Affairs) had agreed to build new township for the inhabitants in the vicinity of Crossroads but in 1983 this was overtaken by a proposal both more ambitiou and more significant to Black urbanisation policy. The plan wa to build a new city of 200-300,000 for all Blacks legally resid- ent in the Cape Town metropolis, at Khayelitsha out on False Ba beyond Mitchells Plain (Figure 7.1). This represented recogni- tion of the permanence of large numbers of Blacks in the Wester Cape (and abandonment of "Coloured labour preference") but in peripheral location. Dissatisfaction on the part of formal town- ship dwellers to the prospect of relocation to Khayelitsha le this element of the plan to be abandoned in 1985; Blacks illeg- ally in Cape Town would, however, be permitted to build shacks a Khayelitsha on site-and-service plots.

Subsequent developments have involved both 'legal' an 'illegal' residents, the former moving into basic 'core' dwel- lings which could subsequently be extended while the latter buil their own. By the end of the first phase in mid-1985 there wer about 13,000 people living in 'core' houses and 30,000 squatter had moved from Crossroads to 4150 site-and-service plots. How- ever, there were riots about forced removals from Crossroads i February 1985, which left 18 dead. And in 1986 more seriou disturbances broke out when conservative Blacks (known a 'witdoeke') clashed with radicals 'comrades', with up to 100 people killed and thousands of shack dwellings destroyed. Ther were suspicions that the authorities had used conflict withir Crossroads to help break up the settlement and encourage moves t Khayelitsha.

The second case of spontaneous settlement is taken from part of one of the 'homelands' - Bophuthatswana (Figure 7.2). It reveals something more of the significance of the 'independence' of the 'Black republics'. The area contains three formal townships - Ga-Rankuwa, Temba and Mabopane - but also a large population of Blacks who have settled spontaneously (though not necessarily illegally) outside the townships. By the time Bophuthatswana was granted its 'independence' it is estimated that there were over 0.33 million 'squatters' in the Winterveld, Klippan and Oskraal areas around the formal townships. Two important features distinguish this situation from that of Blacks in spontaneous settlements within 'White' South Africa. The first is that the settlements are geographically displaced, from the outer edge of the city (in this case Pretoria) to just within the 'homeland'. The second is that these settlements are the responsibility of an 'independent' state. What would otherwise be an expensive inconvenience to 'White' South Africa or the city of Pretoria is thus transferred to a 'foreign country'.

One final feature of urbanisation in contemporary South Africa which deserves attention is the informal sector of the economy. This is closely associated with spontaneous settlement, but has been part of the economic structure of South African cities for a long time. The term informal sector, in its strictest sense, means unlicensed and unrecorded activities. The kind of activities found in the informal sector in South Africa includes retailing (e.g. street peddling, hawking, food stalls, flower sellers, informal drinking places or 'shebeens'), personal services (e.g. shoe repairing, child minding), manufacturing (e.g. building trades, knitting, brewing liquor) and also gambling, drug pushing and prostitution. The informal sector provides many Blacks and some Coloureds and Indians with employment opportunities denied them by the formal sector. As with spontaneous settlement, the authorities tend to discourage the informal sector and support this attitude with fairly strict controls.

Two cases of the informal sector may be described briefly. The first involves an area of spontaneous settlement - Crossroads (Figure 7.3). A recent survey identified 116 businesses here, most of them in retailing with cafes and food shops predominating. Manufacturing activities include the production of clothing, knitwear and tin trunks. Only half the incomes generated reached R200 a month and a quarter less than R100 - figures roughly representative of what might be earned in the mines and domestic service respectively.

The second case is that of Soweto. Surveys suggest that anything from one tenth to one third of households participate in the informal sector. While many traders operate within Soweto, others travel into Johannesburg to sell their wares at the transport termini and other places through which large numbers of Black commuters pass. Informal retailing or hawking is spread all over the township; most of the hawkers sell foodstuffs, and they generally operate from primitive stalls set up daily.

The process of urbanisation is important to South Africa in various ways but most of all because of its involvement of a

68

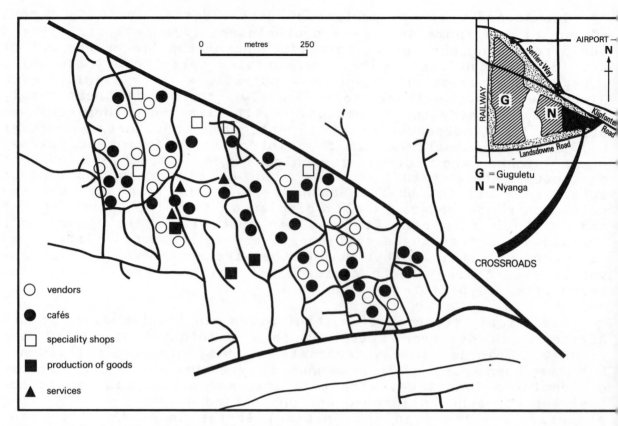

Figure 7.3   The informal sector in Crossroads
              Source: Dewar and Watson (1981, p. 52)

steadily increasing proportion of the Black population. Hal
South Africa's total urban population is now Black and the Huma
Sciences Research Council estimates that if the current rate i
maintained 75 per cent of the Black population will be urbanise
by the end of the century, which means 21 million additiona
Blacks in urban areas by the year 2000.   Not only will Sout
Africa's cities become steadily more Black, but their very for
will increasingly be an outcome of Blacks making their own live
- shelter and work - in an informal process which will becom
ever harder for the authorities to control.

     However, there is a sense in which Black urbanisation migh
be a solution to pressing problems in South Africa.   Populatio
projections by demographers at the Human Sciences Researc
Council in 1986 (and going well beyond those in Table 6.1 above
predict a Black population of 846 million by the year 2100 i
influx control constraining urbanisation continues.   The Whites
along with the Indians and Coloureds, would be a miniscul
minority in the total population (see Table 7.4).   The abolitio
of influx control would reduce the figure to 132 million, bu
this is still much larger than the 80 million people which it i
estimated that South Africa could accommodate.   To restrict th
population to something approximating this figure requires bot
the abolition of influx control and the industrialisation of th
'homelands' or 'national states'.

     This analysis is based on the operation of the demographi
transition, whereby high birth rates and high death rate

Table 7.4   Population projections (millions) based on alterna-
             tive assumptions concerning urbanisation

	1980	2000	2050	2100
Blacks, assuming influx control:				
1 continues	22	37	160	846
2 abolished	22	35	65	132
3 abolished and 'national states' industrialised	22	35	67	73
Whites	4.5	5.3	6.1	6.2
Indians	0.8	1.1	1.5	1.6
Coloureds	2.5	3.6	5.2	5.5

Source: Human Sciences Research Council, **Newsletter** 167, 1986

associated with low levels of economic development are replaced
by continuing high birth rates but lowering death rates as
modernisation takes place (thus increasing natural population
increase), to be followed by falling birth rates with more
advanced economic development.   The key to attainment of the
final stage of low population growth is urban industrialisation,
which encourages material consumption and population control.   In
South Africa the influx control measures designed to prevent
Blacks from swamping the 'White' cities are retarding demographic
changes on which lower rates of population growth depend.   Whereas the average number of children per White woman in South Africa
is approximately two, and for Indians and Coloureds three, it is
between six and seven for Black women in the 'homelands'.   But
for urban Blacks the figure is roughly four.   Without large-scale
migration to the cities, or urban-based industrialisation in the
'homelands', or both, the prospect early in the next century is
for widespread poverty and famine as the Black population continues to climb ever faster.   Even if confined to the periphery,
such conditions could clearly pose a threat to the survival of
the White-controlled core regions of South Africa.

    According to the Human Sciences Research Council, the most
effective strategy for population control involves industry-based
metropolitan growth within or on the borders of the 'homelands'
as well as the continued growth of the existing metropolitan
areas.   The prospect for industrial decentralisation are considered in the next chapter;   attention here is confined to new
developments in urbanisation policy in the heart of the Republic
of South Africa.

    In September 1985 the President's Council published a report on urbanisation strategy, which promised the total abolition of influx control. In April 1986 the infamous Pass Laws responsible for influx control were repealed, a move which was widely if not universely accepted as evidence of real reform of a central pillar of apartheid. In their place the government proposed a policy of 'orderly' (otherwise 'constructive' or 'controlled') urbanisation, which would apply equally to all South Africans and not only to Blacks. The state thus sought to remove the major irritant of the pass system, while still maintaining control of what was likely to be an accelerating process of urbanisation.

When the euphoria surrounding the abolition of the Pass Laws had subsided, it became clear that one system of Black influx control was simply to be replaced by another. The original constraint on urbanisation was exercised through the labour market - through the need for Blacks to qualify for urban resid- ence by employment. The new constraint is exercised through access to housing: new urban residents must obtain approved accommodation, which may be harder to find than employment (the actual search for which may be dependent on having a place to live). Furthermore, the 7.5 million inhabitants of the 'indepen- dent' states of Transkei, Bophuthatswana, Venda and Ciskei not qualifying for South African citizenship are now treated offi- cially as 'aliens' with respect to employment and residence in the Republic of South Africa. Neither this nor the new influx control measures are explicitly racial, but they are clearly designed to keep Blacks out of South Africa's cities.

The new significance attached to accommodation in the cities highlights the growing gap between supply and demand with respect to Black housing. This is illustrated in Table 7.5, which assumes an urbanisation surge in the second half of the 1980s as a result of the 'abolition' of influx control. The first five years of the 1980s saw only 8000 housing units built annually for Blacks in the urban areas, compared with figures of about 260,000, 85,000 and 87,000 a year required in the periods 1985-90, 1990-95 and 1995-2000 respectively, as derived from Table 7.5. For increased state housing construction to bridge this gap is inconceivable. The alternatives are more private sector involvement, which the government is trying to encourage despite limited effective demand on the part of Blacks, and spontaneous settlement which may prove ever harder to control.

Table 7.5 Black housing needs in urban areas 1985-2000

	1985	1990	1995	2000
Black population	5,964,488	13,658,000	16,181,000	18,776,0
Housing units needed	1,004,123	2,299,327	2,724,074	3,160,9
Housing stock 1985	465,901	465,901	465,901	465,9
Cumulative backlog	538,222	1,833,426	2,258,173	2,695,0

Source: National Buildings Research Institute, Pretoria, as reproduced in Business Day, 6 October 1986

Note: Excludes 'homelands'; units needed based on average of 5.94 persons/household

71

e 18   The informal sector of the economy: street-side pur-
        veying of meat in Crossroads.

e 19   A more formal retail outlet in Crossroads: part of a
        'shack' converted for the sale of canned and other
        processed foods.

Plate 20   Home and family of Bophuthatswana factory worker.
Those with jobs in the modern sector of the 'homelands'
economy or commuting across the frontier into 'White'
South Africa form part of an emerging Black 'labour
aristocracy'.

Plate 21   Squatter huts in the Winterveld area of Bophuthatswana,
where spontaneous settlements have sprawled across the
landscape since 'independence'.

8 Development planning

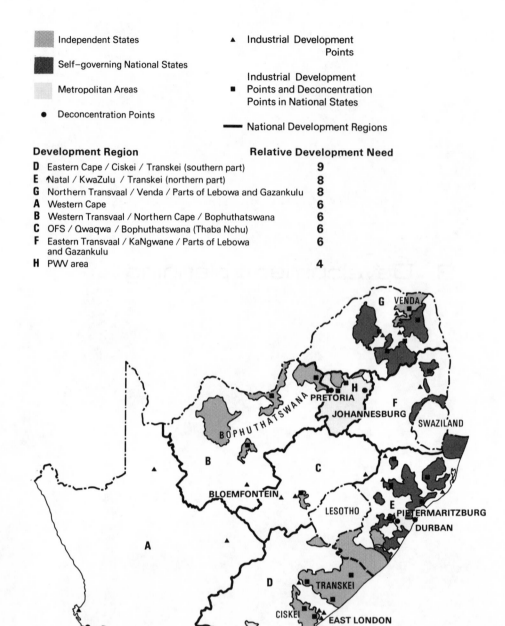

Figure 8.1   Industrial decentralisation and regional development
             strategy 1982
             Source: RSA (1983, p. 946)

8 DEVELOPMENT PLANNING

A fundamental feature of development planning in South Africa is the strategy of 'decentralisation'. Population migration from rural to urban areas, the disproportionate growth of metropolitan regions and an increasingly polarised space economy are features of many countries, developed and underdeveloped, and state planning is usually directed towards stimulation or regeneration of the periphery and imposition of constraints on growth in the core. In South Africa the situation is given special significance by the fact that under apartheid the core is supposed to be White and the periphery Black. The interrelated policies of influx control and decentralisation must therefore be understood in the context of the continuing contradiction between the Whites' need for cheap Black labour and the preservation of racial territorial integrity. This chapter concentrates on those special features of development planning in South Africa which are most relevant to the operation of apartheid.

The need for industrial decentralisation as a strategy for keeping Blacks out of the cities was recognised as soon as the Nationalists came to power. However, government policy was that industrial development within the 'homelands' should be undertaken only with Black capital. Thus the industrial decentralisation programming established in 1960 sought to encourage development in 'border areas' or selected 'White' towns adjoining the 'homelands'. Black labour would be drawn from the 'homelands' for the most part: an early version of the 'frontier commuter'. Indeed, the cheap and plentiful labour provided by the 'homelands', along with financial incentives (e.g. grants towards land, capital and housing costs and tax concessions), was the major attraction to businesses.

The rather modest achievements of the 'border area' strategy led to a change in policy, embodied in the Environmental Planning Act of 1967. This shifted the emphasis to new 'growth points' based on existing towns or cities away from the major industrial concentrations but with more growth potential than the border areas, e.g. Newcastle, Pietersburg and Ladysmith. The policy of disallowing White investment in the 'homelands' was reversed and the government launched a programme of industrial expansion within the 'homelands'. The perceived need for the state to exercise greater control over industrial location in certain large urban areas was expressed in measures which constrained or prevented industrial expansion involving increased employment of Blacks. In addition the government exercised its powers over wage determination and conditions of service to sanction measures which effectively enabled employers to reduce labour costs in 'border areas' and 'homeland' locations.

The two decades 1960-80 saw 113,700 new Black jobs created in enterprises established through the medium of the development corporations responsible for decentralisation, in the 'border areas' and 'homelands'. About 75,000 were in 'border areas', 38 per cent of these adjoining KwaZulu and 26 per cent on the edge of Bophuthatswana. Total investment and associated costs involved in 'border area' development was approximately R1000

millions. The balance of almost 40,000 jobs was in the 'hom
lands'. Against those achievements must be set over 100,000 jo
affected by the refusal of permission for development under t
Environment and Planning Act since 1968, i.e. potential Bla
jobs in the controlled (metropolitan) areas sacrificed as part
the overall decentralisation strategy. These figures suggest
geographical transfer of employment from core to peripher
rather than a net increase of jobs for Blacks in South Africa
a whole.

Table 8.1 shows the distribution of new jobs created in t
'homelands' and 'border areas' over the period 1960-81/2. Almo
half the jobs created within the 'homelands' are
Bophuthatswana, largely in places just inside the portion of t
'homeland' to the north of Pretoria where Babelegi has attract
considerable investment from South African and multination
firms. Most of the remaining jobs are in KwaZulu.

Table 8.1   Industrial employment for Blacks created in 'home-
             lands' and 'border areas' 1960-81/2

'Homeland'	Within 'home-lands' up to March 1981	'Border areas' up to March 1982	Contributi of manufac uring to G (%) 1977
Bophuthatswana	14,555	21,590	10.8
Ciskei	3,076	14,662	8.1
Transkei	no data	0	8.2
Venda	283	417	9.5
Gazankulu	726	734	11.2
KaNgwame	182	1,585	9.6
KwaNdebele	no data		
KwaZulu	7,292	31,866	9.4
Lebowa	3,264	4,803	11.4
Gwaqwa	434	1,201	3.5
Total	29,812	76,858	9.5

Source: RSA (1983, p. 241; 1985, p. 246)

Note: These figures refer to specific government programme
          Other official sources indicate 193,000 jobs 'decer
          tralised' between 1960 and 1981, about 150,000 to growt
          points in 'border areas' or 'homelands' - an average
          7,500 a year compared with 115,000 Blacks entering t
          potential labour force in these areas annually.

The failure of industrial decentralisation to come up to expectations brought a reappraisal of government policy at the beginning of the 1980s. In April 1982 the government published a white paper entitled **The Promotion of Industrial Development: An Element of a Co-ordinated Regional Development Strategy for Southern Africa**, setting out its new policy, arrived at after discussions with the 'homelands'. The essence of the policy is the identification of broad development regions covering the whole of South Africa, and the formulation of 'a coherent regional development strategy, which should be aimed at the exploitation of the full development potential of each region, including agricultural, mining, services and industrial potential' (RSA, 1983, p. 945). This is said to require 'close cooperation between the different states' - i.e. the 'homelands' and 'White' South Africa.

Figure 8.1 illustrates the main feature of the new strategy. Eight major development regions are recognised, taking in 'home-lands' as well as 'White' areas. These are classified according to relative development need, identified by the criterion of need for employment, need for higher standards of living and the potential of the region to satisfy its own employment needs. Five types of areas and/or points are distinguished: (1) metro-politan areas, with the most favourable conditions for industrial development; (2) deconcentration points, adjacent or close to the metropolitan areas, which can be used to lessen the pressure of over-concentration in the metropolitan areas; (3) industrial development points, where alternative agglomeration advantages to those in the metropolitan areas could be created so as to gener-ate employment in the region concerned; (4) other industrial points, with less potential and/or where development needs are not as great as in other areas; (5) **ad hoc** cases, where decen-tralisation incentives may be granted if the authorities so decide. Figure 8.1 shows that the locations chosen for develop-ment under (2), (3) and (4) are for the most part in 'border areas' or just inside 'homelands', i.e. they follow a pattern similar to that of the earlier policy. Various financial incen-tives apply in these locations, to compensate for cost disadvan-tages, provide for utilities, house key personnel, and so on. Within the metropolitan areas industrial development will be con-trolled, but more selectively than in the past. To implement the new programmes the budget for decentralisation was doubled to a figure exceeding R100 millions.

Three important features of the new strategy should be recog-nised. The first is that its basic intent is the same as before: to keep Blacks out of the major cities as far as possible, while at the same time facilitating their employment, hence the con-tinuing emphasis on 'border area' locations and growth points just within the 'homelands'. The second feature is a recognition in the white paper that the economic potential of some regions is largely of a non-industrial nature and that agriculture, mining and other forms of development would have to receive highest priority. The third and most significant feature is that South Africa is viewed as an economically integrated territory, in which the Black 'national states' or 'republics' are subsumed within the major development regions: political 'independence' clearly does not entail an independent economic identity for the 'homelands'.

Decentralisation is an important element in the broade
strategy whereby the South African government seeks to implemer
a particular pattern of spatial organisation. Apartheid ideolo
must somehow resolve the contradiction between the reality o
economic interdependence and the political independence which th
'homelands' are supposed to possess. A 'constellation' or cor
federation of states was put forward in 1979 by P. W. Botha
whereby an institutional framework would be established fo
cooperation on all matters of common concern. Transkei
Bophuthatswana, Venda and Ciskei are viewed as obvious candidate
for membership of such a constellation. In South Africa's offi
cial view, these 'republics' now have the same political statu
as Botswana, Lesotho and Swaziland, which form part of a custon
union with South Africa. The remaining Black 'independer
states' might join the confederation at a later stage. Such
proposal echoes earlier South African aspirations of leadir
neighbouring Black states towards a mutually beneficial an
harmonious future through economic interdependence. Eight year
later, no firm proposals have yet been made to involve the 'home
lands' directly in the affairs of the 'White' republic.

There is an alternative view of the emerging economic an
political geography of South (and southern) Africa, however
This sees its purpose as, first and foremost, ensuring the per
petuation of a White-controlled, prosperous capitalist economy i
the Republic of South Africa. Francis Wilson, a University o
Cape Town economist, has likened the political economy o
southern Africa to an onion, with a central core surrounded by
number of rings. The central core represents the mines an
factories, towns and cities of South Africa surrounded by th
'White' farming areas. The first ring around this core repre
sents the non-independent 'homelands', the second the 'indeper
dent homelands', the next the former High Commission Territorie
of Botswana, Lesotho and Swaziland, and finally the state
beyond. Each of the layers has a successively greater degree o
formal political independence from South Africa. Wilson relate
those political entities to labour links. For much of thi
century the political boundaries separating the different layer
from the core were not particularly significant: South Afric
drew its labour, in the form of migrants, from large parts o
southern Africa with little trouble. As political change too
place to the north, with countries in the outer layers peelir
off in so far as South Africa's **de facto** control was concernec
dependence on foreign migrants has been reduced (as shown i
Chapter 6). Now the emphasis has shifted to reinforcing boundar
ies closer to the core. The problems of population growth
unemployment and poverty in the 'homelands' are externalised b
'independence' and a restructuring of influx control. The chea
labour produced in the 'homelands' is admitted to the core a
demand requires, through the medium of frontier commuting as wel
as migrant workers. Once in the core, the mobility of worker
between sectors and localities is facilitated by reforms o
legislation governing Black labour affairs (initiated by th
Wiehahn and Riekert Commissions - two major government enquirie
conducted at the end of the 1970s with a view to making th
employment of Black labour more effective). Those Blacks wh
are, in effect, permanent residents of the core of 'White' Sout
Africa have their status recognised by the possibility of hon

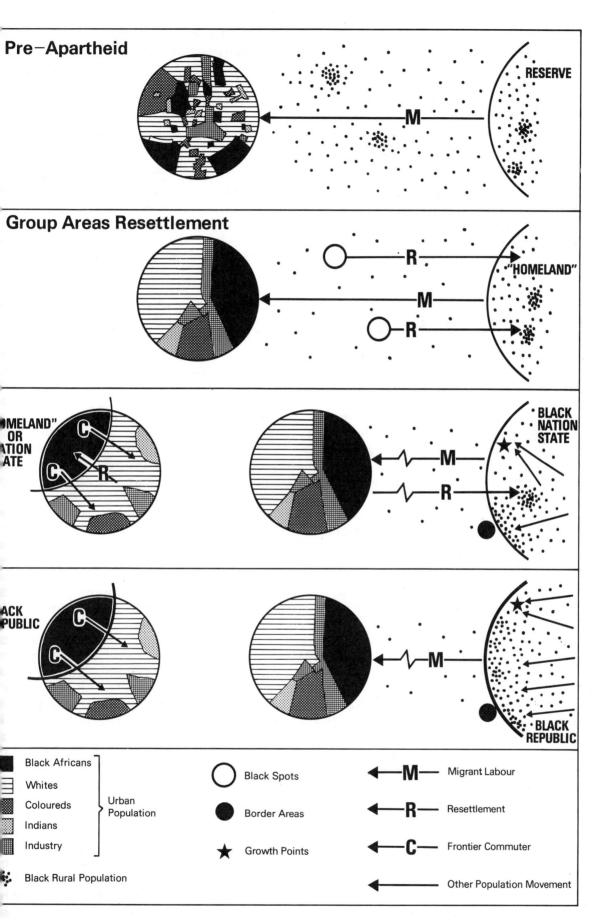

Figure 8.2   Stages in the development of apartheid planning
Source: suggested in part by Western (1981, p. 65)

ownership; they thus become a kind of lower labour aristocracy
with levels of living conspicuously superior to that of Blacks i
the 'homeland' labour reserves but inferior to that of the Whit
working class (higher labour aristocracy) whose continuing sup
port for the government is based on economic advantage associate
with racial superiority.

Wilson's analogy helps, again, to see the emerging role c
the 'homelands' in a broader context. Both the partial externa
lisation of labour costs and effective influx control are facili
tated by 'independence', which is in this sense not the fictio
which some opponents of apartheid claim. It serves a specifi
purpose more effectively than if these territories were politi
cally integral to the Republic of South Africa. The continuatio
of this role depends on 'homeland' leadership compliant wit
South Africa's purpose (if they have any choice), at least in th
'independent republics', and this is being assisted by the emer
gence of a property-owning middle class supportive of the **statu
quo**. As far as the independent neighbouring states are cor
cerned, eg Zimbabwe, Botswana and Namibia (occupied by Sout
Africa), the strategy is one of perpetuating economic dependence
with armed force and 'destabilisation' as fall-backs if Sout
Africa sees itself seriously threatened.

In conclusion, it may be suggested that apartheid as
spatial planning strategy has proceeded through a number o
distinct stages since the Nationalists came to power. The essen
tial features are sketched out in Figure 8.2. Stage 1 shows th
pre-apartheid pattern of ethnic diversity with some segregatio
in the cities, a large and scattered Black population in th
countryside, and a traditional subsistence economy in th
reserves which were connected to the cities by migrant labou
flows. Stage 2 shows the tidying up of the social geography c
the cities by the Group Areas Act and the resettlement of urba
and rural Blacks into what were now deemed to be their periphera
'homelands'. In stage 3 there is a distinction between two kind
of cities - those in which the Black townships can be assigned t
nearby 'homelands' with their residents becoming 'frontier com
muters' (e.g. Durban) and those too far from the 'homelands
(e.g. Johannesburg) where the Black labour force must be migran
or, in effect, permanent. In stage 3 the tidying-up of th
countryside continues, by eliminating 'black spots' and further
ing 'homeland' consolidation. Stage 4 shows the borders betwee
'White' South Africa and the 'homelands' strengthened by th
granting of independence; this is no impediment, however, to th
planning of an integrated economic system as represented by th
continuation of decentralisation via growth points straddling th
borders.

Thus far, this evolving strategy has been successful i
maintaining South Africa as a White-controlled capitalis
country. Whether it remains so will depend not only on th
system's capacity to keep at bay the increasing peripheral popu
lation of poor Blacks, but also on its ability to resolve tensio
arising in the core from the imperative of employing Black labou
without conceding political power, i.e. to control interna
dissent. The next two chapters review the state of unrest, an
the process of 'reform' whereby apartheid is being adapted t
changing conditions.

9 Unrest

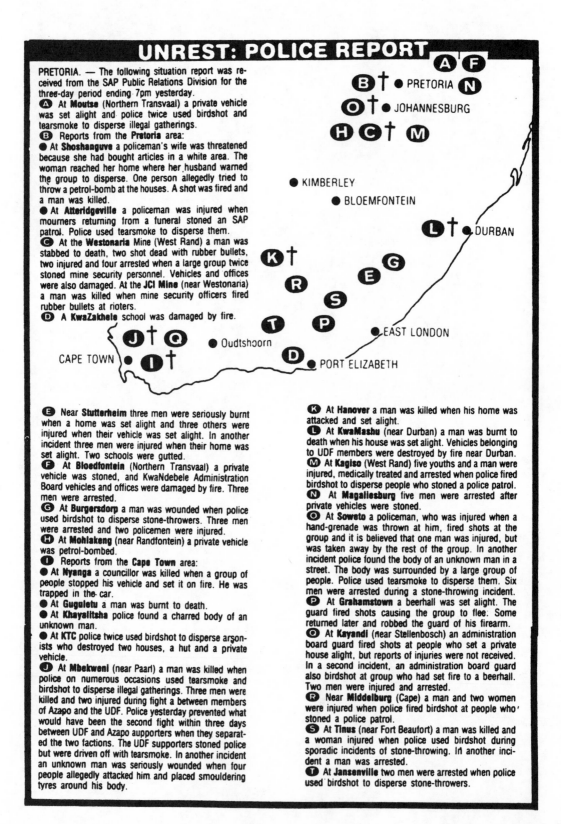

Not a happy Christmas for some South Africans: police reports of unrest for December 24, 25 and 26, 1985, as reproduced in **The Cape Times**, 27 December 1985. By Christmas 1986 the authorities were not permitting the publication of such details, but reported seven Black 'politically related' deaths over the Christmas period, including three shot in a township clash with police and three killed in conflict among Blacks.

9 UNREST

That apartheid should be accompanied by social unrest is hardly surprising. However, there is more to unrest than the drama of confrontations between Blacks and the South African police or security forces which tend to dominate media coverage. The way in which unrest is expressed also includes less conspicuous but possibly more effective acts of civil disobedience or dissent manifest both in mass boycotts of schools, buses and businesses and in individual challenges to authority or some symbol of oppression. At the other extreme, unrest can involve sabotage, urban 'terrorism' and the 350 or so armed insurgency attacks reported over the past decade. The origin of unrest is also more complex than is often supposed, with important implications for the possible trajectory of change.

While social unrest has for long been an ongoing feature of life under apartheid, it is the major incidents that attract most attention. The first such event was at the township of Sharpeville on the edge of Vereeniging on 21 March 1960 when a peaceful demonstration against the Pass Laws ended in the police shooting into a crowd, leaving 69 Blacks dead and 178 wounded. The months that followed saw a further 83 civilians along with 3 policemen killed, and 365 civilians and 59 police injured, in riots in various towns. A state of emergency was declared, mass detentions were used for the first time, and the African National Congress (ANC) which had for many years led the Black political struggle for civil rights was 'banned' (i.e. declared illegal). The 'Sharpeville massacre' has influenced foreign attitudes to South Africa ever since.

The second major incident, or series of incidents, of violent unrest was associated with Soweto in 1976. Black discontent over the use of Afrikaans as a compulsory medium of instruction in schools culminated in police firing on children on 16 June, setting in motion further unrest which was to leave about 350 dead on the Witwatersrand (Figure 9.1). Violence spread to Coloured areas of Cape Town, where about 130 died - most of them shot by the police. Figure 9.1 shows that the incidents of unrest in Cape Town were spatially restricted to the Coloured residential areas, but, unlike Soweto, they were close enough to where Whites lived to cause unease. There were further serious outbreaks in 1980, coinciding with the anniversary of the 1976 shootings in Soweto, but in this case events began in the Cape and then spread to the Witwatersrand.

The latest period of unrest began in September 1984 and has continued ever since. The immediate precipitating events were riots in Sharpeville and Johannesburg townships over rent increases, which resulted in about 30 deaths. By the end of 1984 there were 149 deaths officially recorded in 'political violence', in 1985 there were 879, and in 1986 a further 1300. As confrontation between Blacks and the police and security forces escalated, accompanied by growing conflict among Blacks (including a clash between Indians and Blacks near Durban in August which left 50 dead), a state of emergency was imposed in Johannesburg and the Eastern Cape in June 1985, later extended to

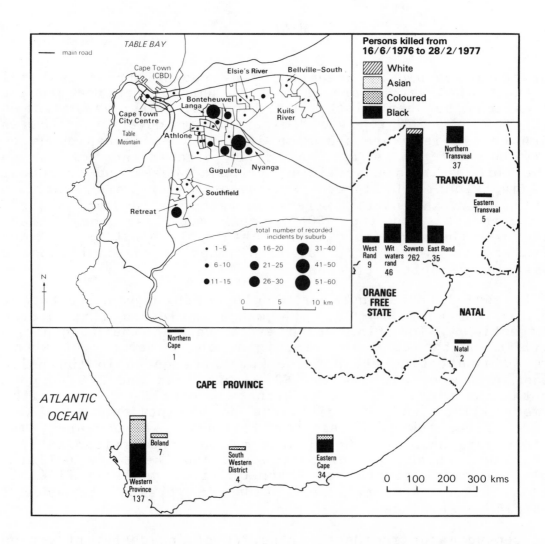

Figure 9.1   The patterns of unrest in 1976, showing those killed
from 16 June 1976 to 28 February 1977 nationally, and
the location of incidents in Cape Town
Source: National map from Readers' Digest **Atlas of
Southern Africa** (1984, p. 34);   Cape Town from Smith
(1982, p. 225)

the Western Cape.   It was lifted in March 1986, but as violent
deaths increased (to 214 in May), a national state of emergency
was declared on 12 June 1986 along with restrictions on the
reporting of unrest.   Severe press censorship was imposed later
in 1986, since when the nature and extent of unrest is a matter
more of speculation than accurate reporting.

During much of 1985 and 1986 the **Cape Times** published an
'unrest map' along with the daily police reports (see page 82)
and this source provides a detailed indication of what has actually been taking place.   Table 9.1 lists the types of incidents
and locations involved in one particular month.   Violent unrest
usually took the form of a group of Blacks or, less often,
Coloureds, throwing stones at vehicles or attacking buildings
with petrol bombs.   The targets were usually the South African
police or defence force or institutions and individuals viewed as
agents of repression.   Schools were frequently attacked, sometimes by their own increasingly politicised students, as were
homes and vehicles of Black policemen and local councillors, and

Table 9.1   Unrest in South Africa, September 1985

Type of incident		Number
Attacks on vehicles:	police and SA defence force	60
	private	34
	other public and commercial	69
Attacks on buildings:	private homes	38
	schools	28
	commercial	15
	police premises	4
	other public facilities	10
Other stone throwing		28
Other violence, attacks or use of unspecified force		20
Barricades erected		10
Other arson or explosions		6
Robbery associated with unrest		5
Police use of firearms		47
Other use of firearms		5
Police use of teargas/smoke		11
Arrests, including multiples, of:	Blacks	134
	Coloureds	45
Attacks on, injuries or woundings of:	Blacks	63
	Coloureds	8
	Whites	5
	Indians	1
	Police and SADF	25
Deaths:	Blacks killed by police action	13
	Other Black deaths	19
	Coloureds	2
	Police (Black)	2

Type of location	Number
Black townships in 'White' South Africa	165
Black townships in 'homelands'	7
Black spontaneous settlements	2
Mines	4
Coloured residential areas	45
White areas	12
Unidentified	6

Source: South African Police daily reports, as reproduced in the **Cape Times**

Note: There is usually more than one incident reported at each location.

of two Coloured members of parliament. The police reponse was usually to move in with force, thus provoking further violent response, and to use shotguns resulting in injuries to demonstrators. The number of Blacks killed by police action may have been larger than the 13 reported by the police themelves; there is no independent corroboration. Most of the other 19 deaths were attributed to the action of Blacks on other Blacks, including five burned to death in 'necklace' killings. This form of retribution, which involves placing a burning tyre around the victim's neck, has become almost a ritualised means of disposing of those considered to be informers or otherwise deeply implicated with the forces of the state.

The types of locations involved show that the pressure poin
are predominantly the Black townships in 'White' South Afric
The spontaneous settlements generated only two recorded inciden
of violence in this month. Mine compounds were the scene of fo
outbreaks: it is here that violence often finds its most brut
expression, among men living in dormitories away from the
families and with sufficient tribal loyalty for frustration
lead to vicious faction fights. The Coloured areas in the Ca
erupted periodically, twice in September 1985, with a violen
characteristic of that reported day-to-day in the Black tow
ships. White places and people experienced very little of t
violence, and the Indians, it would appear, even less.

Violent confrontation is by no means the only strategy
opposition to White domination. There have been massive no
violent protests focussed on specific issues: rent boycotts
response to the raising of rentals on overcrowded accommodati
of poor quality, boycotts of buses stimulated by fare increas
exacerbating the discomfort of long distance commuting fr
peripheral townships, and a widespread stay-away from schoo
seen to provide inadequate education. There have also be
boycotts of White businesses. An increase in strikes by Blac
is a further manifestation of unrest. The funerals of tho
killed in demonstrations have provided effective venues for ma
expressions of Black solidarity as well as of grief.

The South African authorities attempt to portray unrest in
manner consistent with their own view of the world. Sta
President P. W. Botha has been quoted as saying that there is
racial strife: 'The struggle in South Africa is not a strugg
between Black and White but between democratic institutions a
communist dictatorship'. Those responsible for unrest are se
as a small radical (or Marxist) minority. Great emphasis
placed on violence by Blacks on Blacks, which the government
figures show to be responsible for more deaths in recent mont
than the police and defence forces.

However, there are deeper structural causes. The Sou
African Institute of Race Relations identified the crisis
Black education (under-resourced and repressive), the econom
situation (with rising unemployment) and the new constitution
underlying causes of the disturbances in 1984 which precipitat
the current period of unrest. These exacerbate the appalli
living conditions that millions of blacks endure in townships a
squatter camps. And the response is purposeful rather th
indiscriminate, usually involving the deliberate targetting
persons or property seen to be part of a system of repressio
Where the South African government is right, and right to be ve
concerned indeed, is that the struggle is no longer exclusive
racial. The growing antagonism between political radicalism (
exemplified by the re-emergence of the ANC as a potent politic
force and more conservative elements (exemplified by Chi
Buthelezi of KwaZulu's Inkatha movement) is a major issue fr
which social unrest arises and which it seeks to resolve. Blac
are increasingly seeing an exploitive capitalist economy as we
as a repressive White political system as the source of the
subjugation.

10 The 'reform' of apartheid

The African National Congress (ANC) celebrated its 75th anniversary in 1987. Its emergence in the 1950s as a mass movement peacefully advocating one-man-one-vote in South Africa owed much to the Black lawyer Nelson Mandela. The ANC was 'banned' following the Sharpeville shootings in 1960. In 1961 Mandela became leader of Umkhonto we Siswe ('Spear of the Nation'), the newly-formed military wing of the ANC. In 1964 he was imprisoned for life, but became a potent symbol of the Black liberation struggle. The ANC has greatly increased its influence in recent years as a rallying force for Black opposition to White rule. The ANC's aims are broadly shared by the United Democratic Front (UDF), a loose multi-racial affiliation of groups initially brought together to oppose the new constitution.

10 THE 'REFORM' OF APARTHEID

partheid is dead - or so some leading Nationalist politicians
re asserting. Early in 1984 the Deputy Minister of Foreign
ffairs, Louis Nel, claimed that apartheid as perceived by the
utside world no longer existed in the hearts and minds of most
eople in South Africa, and was in this sense dead. Opening
arliament on 31 January 1986, State President Botha stated that
outh Africans had outgrown 'the outdated concept of apartheid'.
wo days later, in a prominent newspaper advertisement, he
nnounced that he and his government were committed to power-
haring, equal opportunity for all, equal treatment, and equal
ustice.

The 'reform' of apartheid, if not its complete abolition, has
een very much part of the debate on South Africa in recent
ears. Great expectations have been aroused, and significant
chievements noted. The South African Institute of Race Rela-
ions **Quarterly Countdown** (No 3, 1986) observed as follows:

Twenty years after the assisination of Dr Verwoerd (6
September 1966) South Africa has changed in ways that
then seemed unthinkable. Black unions now have statu-
tory status. Parliament has been partially desegregate,
the policy of starving Black education has been
reversed, social desegregation is occurring, the pass
laws have been repealed, and the permanence of urban
Africans has been accepted.

n another issue (No 2, 1986) they state:

During the second quarter of 1986 the tricameral parliament enacted the most far-reaching reforms in South
Africa since the National Party's election victory in
1948. They include the repeal of the pass laws, the
granting of freehold rights to Africans, and provision
for South African citizenship to be regained by Africans
who had been denationalised. In addition, fully multi-
racial executive government was instituted at provincial
level, though on a nominated basis only.

hile reminding readers that one in every three Africans (Blacks)
ad been deprived of South African citizenship through the
independent homelands' policy, that hundreds of thousands of
lacks had been forcibly removed from their homes, and that race
till forms the basis even for some new administrative measures,
he Institute was clearly reflecting the contemporary reformist
limate.

What substance is there to claim that apartheid is being
eformed, or even that it is dead? Have major changes in the
irection of racial equality been made, with others on the way?
o what extent is the government taking the lead, rather than
eing forced into reforms by internal dissent and external pres-
ure? Could it be that the term apartheid is now an embarrass-
ent, but that the Whites are merely restructuring a system of
acial domination to make it more effective (and possibly less

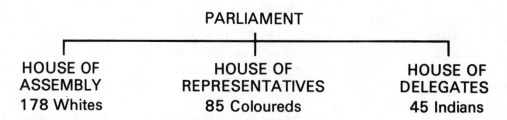

STATE PRESIDENT & CABINET (multiracial)

PARLIAMENT

HOUSE OF ASSEMBLY	HOUSE OF REPRESENTATIVES	HOUSE OF DELEGATES
178 Whites	85 Coloureds	45 Indians

Own Affairs: MINISTERIAL COUNCIL for each House
General Affairs: JOINT COMMITTEES with members from each House

PRESIDENTIAL COUNCIL
35 elected (20 Whites, 10 Coloureds, 5 Indians)
25 nominated (including 6 Whites, 3 Coloureds, 1 Indian)

Figure 10.1 Basic elements of the new constitution introduced in 1984

offensive)? These are some of the questions to be considered briefly here.

The present period of 'reform' began with the initiation of the new constitution in 1984. This provides for a parliament with three houses - for the Whites, Coloureds and Indians respectively (Figure 10.1). A distinction is made between 'general affairs' affecting all race groups, which are considered in all three houses, and 'own affairs' which are the subject of debate only in the house of the group concerned. Affairs deemed to be 'general' are supposed to be resolved by concensus, making use of joint committees comprising members of each house. If no concensus can be reached the final decision is made by the President's Council, on which a White majority is guaranteed by representation and the President's power of nomination.

The major innovation of the new constitution was the incorporation of Coloureds and Indians, including their representation in both cabinet and Presidential Council. However, racial separation is a central feature of the structure, reinforced by the concept of 'own affairs' (which include matters relating to social services, recreational and cultural facilities, housing, community development and local government). The system lacks legitimacy to many Coloureds and Indians; only 31 per cent of the formers' electors and 20 per cent of the latters' voted in the first election to their new houses in 1984. And there is no place in the new parliament for Blacks/Africans.

Subsequent developments have sought to incorporate Blacks and to bring reform into other levels of government and administration. A National Council has been proposed as a means of involving Blacks nationally, via representatives of the 'homelands', and possibly of townships in 'White' South Africa which could become autonomous 'city states' with greater control over their own affairs. New councils for the provinces of Cape, Natal, Orange Free State and Transvaal have nominated representatives of non-white groups. Regional service councils are to bring together representatives of local (racially separate) local authorities on multi-racial bodies concerned with the provision of certain services, and also with aspects of development planning.

While these developments certainly represent some relaxation of White monopoly over decision-making at all levels, they nevertheless retain the basic geo-political structure of 'White' South Africa, Black 'homelands' and racially homogenous local communities. A more radical alternative emerged in 1986 from the so-called KwaZulu-Natal 'Indaba' (conference), involving discussions between Whites, Indians and Blacks, which proposed what was, in effect, a merger of 'White' Natal and the KwaZulu 'homeland' under a constitution which could bring Black majority rule. Government opposition to something so clearly inconsistent with their conception of power-sharing has been made clear. Meanwhile, the policy of 'homeland' independence remains, although the granting of 'republic' status to Kwa Ndebele expected in December 1986, has been postponed.

Evidence of reforms, or at least relaxation of apartheid, is more convincing at the 'petty' and local scale. Formal job reservation has gone, except in the mines (where its abolition is imminent) and racial differences in pay are being phased out. Facilities such as hotels, restaurants, cinemas, buses and beaches have been widely desegregated, with individual local authorities taking the initiative in forcing central government's hand. The concept of 'local option' on these forms of separation is gaining ground. Having for some years required sport to be of 'international' standing for it to be multi-racial, the government is now prepared to accept this at the school level, though schools will still be racially exclusive (except private schools which may chose to admit children irrespective of race).

The 'group areas' concept is beginning to yield to both local pressure and individual action. Early in 1986 the central business districts of Durban and Johannesburg were proclaimed free trading areas for all races, and by the end of the year many other cities had followed. Residential segregation is openly disregarded in some parts of some cities: at the end of 1986, 30,000 people were reported to be living in 'disqualified areas' in Johannesburg, including 9,000 Coloureds, 6,000 Indians and 5,000 Blacks along with the 65,000 Whites in the inner areas of Hillbrow, Berea and Joubert Park. Racially mixed areas have also developed in Cape Town, Durban and Port Elizabeth. Publication of a President's Council report on the Group Areas Act was postponed in late 1986, amidst speculation that recommendations accepting existing mixed or 'grey' areas and proposing the opening up of others went too far for the government. The immediate

prospect is for further **de facto** local options, turning a blin
eye to desegregation in more liberal towns and cities, while th
Act will continue to be rigidly enforced in more conservativ
places.

   The overall impression, at the beginning of 1987, is c
substantial change in some of the details of apartheid, but wit
the government responding to pressure and necessity rather tha
taking a positive lead. Nationalist thinking remains racial
however, and Verwoerd's grand design for national politica
separation little changed. It is accepted that Blacks in larg
numbers are a permanent feature of the Republic's population, ar
that some integration is an inevitable consequence, but for th
Nationalists, continued White rule is non-negotiable and one
man-one-vote inconceivable. The situation has been summarise
thus by Dr F. van Zyl Slabbert, former leader of the oppositio
Progressive Federal Party (**Financial Mail**, 29 August 1986):

> The government has accepted that it cannot **separate** away
> those who are not white from its own position of domina-
> tion. Now it seeks ways to **integrate** them without
> losing its position of domination. Before, it tried for
> separation and White domination, now it tries for integ-
> ration and White domination. ... government at first
> wanted to creat a multi-cultural society through separa-
> tion; it is now prepared to create a multi-racial
> society through integration. ... it first tried to
> exclude and divide and rule; now it is prepared to
> **include** and divide and rule.

The process of inclusion relates not only to the formal positio
of the Coloureds and Indians, and at some future date the Blacks
within new political institutions, but also the co-option of
compliant middle class from members of these groups.

   The crucial question is whether the government has the tim
required for its own form of social and political reconstruction
Its 'reforms' have done little if anything to satisfy Blac
aspirations, and a White right-wing backlash is evident in th
rise of the Conservative Party and the emergence of the neo
fascist Afrikaans Resistance Movement. The general election (fo
Whites) called in 1987 was seen as a necessary test of suppor
for Botha's strategy of limited 'reforms' and a toughening stanc
on internal dissent. Meanwhile, external pressure mounts, in th
form of sanctions and disinvestment. And within the township
radical forces including the ANC are becoming an increasingl
potent movement for changes more fundamental than many libera
opponents of apartheid can contemplate, far less endorse. Th
only certainty in a highly volatile situation is that th
Nationalist government will not yield power to Blacks, and tha
it will retain those elements of apartheid judged necessary t
ensure White survival. That Blacks are increasingly takin
matters into their own hands makes for hard times ahead, for al
South Africans.

Bibliography and sources

BIBLIOGRAPHY AND SOURCES

There are numerous books and articles on South Africa, of varyin
quality and from different disciplinary perspectives.   Wha
follows is confined to geographical literature of recent origi
which provides an up-to-date view, or material of particula
relevance to recent developments.   Also included are reference
to the main sources from which information included in thi
UpDate has been derived.

BIBLIOGRAPHY

Beavon, K.S.O. (1982)   Black Townships in South Africa
                               Terra Incognita for Urban Geogr
                               aphers, **South African Geographica**
                               Journal, 64 (1), pp. 3-2C

Beavon, K.S.O. and   Trekking on: Recent Trends in the
Rogerson, C.M. (1981)   Human Geography of Southern Africa
                               Progress in Human Geography, 5
                               pp. 159-89

Cooke, G. P. (1986)   Khayelitsha - Policy Change o
                               Crisis Response?   **Transactions**
                               Institute of British Geographers
                               11(1), pp. 57-66

Crush, J., Reitsma, H. and   **Decolonizing the Human Geography of**
Rogerson, C. (eds) (1982)   **Southern Africa**, special issue o
                               Tijdschrift voor Economische e
                               Sociale Geografie, 73(4)

Dewar, D. and Ellis, G.   **Low Income Housing Policy in South**
(1979)   **Africa, with Particular Reference t**
                               the Western Cape, Urban Problem
                               Research Unit, University of Cap
                               Town

Dewar, D. and Watson, V.   **Unemployment and the Informal**
(1981)   **Sector: Some Proposals**, Urba
                               Problems Research Unit, Universit
                               of Cape Town (summarised in Smith
                               1982, pp. 124-42)

Ellis, G., Hendrie, D.,   **The Squatter Problem in the Western**
Kooy, A. & Maree, J. (1977)   **Cape: Some Causes and Remedies**
                               South African Institute of Rac
                               Relations, Johannesburg

Fair, T.J.D. (1982)   **South Africa: Spatial Frameworks fo**
                               Development, Juta & Co., Cape Town

Fair, T.J.D. and   The Urbanisation Process in South
Browett, J.G. (1979)   Africa, in D.T. Herbert and R.J
                               Johnston (eds), **Geography and th**
                               Urban Environment, John Wiley
                               Winchester, pp. 259-94

aines, R. and Buijs, G.
eds) (1985)

The Struggle for Social and Economic Space: Urbanization in Twentieth Century South Africa, Institute for Social and Economic Research, University of Durban - Westville

DAF (1983)

Apartheid: The Facts, International Defence and Aid Fund for Southern Africa, London

emon, A. (1976)

Apartheid: A Geography of Separation, Saxon House, Farnborough, Hants.

aasdorp, G. and Pillay, N.
1977)

Urban Relocation and Racial Segregation: The Case of Indian South Africans, Department of Economics, University of Natal, Durban

cCarthy, J. J. and
mith, D. P. (1984)

South African City: Theory in Analysis and Planning, Juta & Co, Cape Town

'Keefe, P. (ed) (1983)

South Africa in the Global Division of Labor, special issue of Antipode, 15(2)

mond, R. (1986)

The Apartheid Handbook, Penguin, Harmondsworth

SA (annual)

South Africa, Official Yearbook of the Republic of South Africa, Chris van Rensburg, Johannesburg

ogerson, C. M. (ed) (1986)

South Africa: Geography in State of Emergency, special issue of GeoJournal, 12(2).

ogerson, C.M. and
eavon, K.S.O. (1980)

The Awakening of 'Informal Sector' Studies in Southern Africa, The South African Geographical Journal, 62(2), pp. 175-90

mit, P. (ed) (1985)

Black Urbanisation, special issue of RSA 2000, Human Science Research Council, Pretoria, 7(1)

mith, D.M. (1977)

Human Geography: A Welfare Approach Edward Arnold, London, Ch. 9

mith, D.M. (ed) (1982)

Living under Apartheid: Aspects of Urbanization and Social Change in South Africa. Allen and Unwin, London

mith, D. M. (1987)

Geography, Inequality and Society, Cambridge University Press, Cambridge, Ch. 6

SAIRR (annual)	**Survey of Race Relations in Sou** **Africa**, South African Institute Race Relations, Johannesburg
Walt, E. (1982)	**South Africa - A Land Divided**, Bla Sash, Johannesburg
Wellings, P. (ed) (1986)	**Southern Africa: The Developme** **Crisis**, special issue of **Geogoru** 17(2)
Welling, P. and Black, A. (1986)	Industrial Decentralisation under Apartheid: The Relocation Industry to the South Afric Periphery, **World Development**, 14(1 pp. 1-38
Western, J. (1981)	**Outcast Cape Town**, Allen and Unwi London

SOURCES

Most of the material presented in the Tables and Figures in th
publication comes from official sources, usually those of t
South African government. Much of this, along with other val
able material, is collected together in two secondary source
published annually, cited above as RSA and SAIRR.

The South African Institute of Race Relations (SAIRR) publishes
monthly **Race Relations News** and regular reports. A subscripti
to the Institute (PO Box 97, Johannesburg 2000, RSA) is an effe
tive means of keeping up with events in South Africa.

The **International Defence and Aid Fund for Southern Africa** pu
lishes regular reports on aspects of apartheid (from Can
Collins House, 64 Essex Road, London N1 81T).

The government of the Republic of South Africa produces a month
South Africa Newsletter and various 'Political Backgrounders
available from the South African Embassy (Trafalgar Squar
London WC2N 5DP) free of charge. This material conveys t
official government view, understanding of which is an importa
part of the study of apartheid.

Hardly a day goes by without some news item on South Africa
The Guardian, The Independent, The Telegraph or **The Times**, a
The Economist also carries regular reports. Weekly press diges
are available: **South African Pressclips** (from 36 Woodside Roa
Tamboerskloof, Cape Town 8C01, RSA) and **South African Dige**
(Bureau for Information, Private Bag X745, Pretoria, RSA) whi
reflects the government's line.

Occasional papers on South African topics appear in Briti
geographical periodicals, including **The Geographical Magazin**
but most useful in this respect is **The South African Geographic**
Journal.